# GOD,
# I WANT A
# REFUND

PALMETTO
PUBLISHING
Charleston, SC
www.PalmettoPublishing.com

Paperback ISBN: 9798822959996

# GOD, I WANT A REFUND

## ROBERT ALLEN

# CONTENTS

# INTRODUCTION

It all began with a simple thought: "Is this really it?" Does life really have to be this complicated? It wasn't a lack of faith but rather a deep desire for understanding. Why do bad things happen to good people? Why is suffering a part of existence?

When I say, "God, I want a refund," what I mean is that it's OK to send something back and ask for a refund if you don't like it. You don't have to accept something you don't like. With that being said, if you're not happy with a current situation in your life, whether it is your health, your job, your finances, or your relationship, it's OK to say, "God, I would like a refund." Send it back and ask for something better in your life.

For example, if you order a steak with a baked potato and steamed vegetables at a restaurant and they bring you out cold chicken nuggets and French fries, you're not expected to eat it or pay for it. Why would you settle for cold chicken nuggets in your life when you've ordered a T-bone or rib eye steak?

If you order my book, *God, I Want a Refund*, online and they send you a copy of a different book you already have on your bookshelf, it's OK to keep the book. If you want to, you can gift it to somebody. You can choose to reread it, or you can make a choice to send it back and get a refund. You have the power and the right to reclaim your life, make changes, and pursue what truly aligns with your desires and values. You deserve to enjoy the life you've worked so hard for and not settle for less. If something doesn't meet your expectations, don't shy away from demanding what you deserve. Remember, it's about seeking the fulfillment you rightfully want, just as you would in any other aspect of life.

If you start acknowledging what you truly deserve, you begin to change your reality. When you demand more of yourself and the world around you, you open doors to new opportunities and growth. Transforming your mindset can lead to a cascade of positive changes.

This book can aid you in rediscovering your potential, identifying what brings you happiness, and reclaiming your sense of purpose for those changes. Let it serve as a tool to remind you of your worth and the possibilities that lie ahead.

# PROLOGUE

It started on a quiet evening when I found myself reflecting on my health struggles. The day's fatigue weighed on me, and I reached for a pen and paper, intending to jot down some ideas on managing my well-being. The simple act of writing felt therapeutic, a way to make sense of the challenges I faced daily.

As the pen moved across the pages, I found myself diving deeper, not just into my health but into the broader canvas of my life. I wrote about the lessons I had learned, the resilience I had developed, and the ways I had overcome the odds. I recalled moments of triumph and despair, each memory a stepping stone in my journey.

Days turned into weeks, and what started as a few notes evolved into a comprehensive exploration of my experiences. I realized I wasn't just documenting strategies for better health; I was unraveling the wisdom I had gained from a life filled with trials and triumphs. The pages multiplied, filled with stories of overcoming childhood circumstances, rebuilding relationships, and finding strength amid adversity.

One evening as I reread my writings, a realization struck me. My reflections were more than personal experiences; they were a guide that could help others navigate their own challenges. Inspired, I decided to compile my insights into a book. I envisioned it as a beacon of hope for those struggling with similar issues, a tribute to the power of resilience and the human spirit.

My book took shape, chapter by chapter, each one a piece of my heart and soul. I wrote about my father's addiction and our eventual reconciliation, about the importance of mutual respect in relationships, and about the healing power of forgiveness. My words were raw and honest, a testament to my journey and a gift to anyone who might find solace in them.

As I neared the completion of my book, I felt a profound sense of purpose. I hoped that my book would touch at least one person, offering them the courage and insight to overcome their own struggles. And in that hope, I found fulfillment, knowing that my life's experiences had the potential to light the way for others.

# CHAPTER 1
## HEALTH

Life's trials began to feel like an endless series of unfair tests. The prayers seemed unanswered, the dreams unfulfilled. I wondered: is this really my life now? The sense of injustice and futility bloomed into a vivid mix of frustration and sadness, coloring daily existence with no end in sight.

I had felt unwell for many years. I felt like I'd tried everything. I went to every specialist, including the Mayo Clinic. I googled every symptom over and over again. I became consumed with being sick; it completely took over my life, and I was slowly becoming a hypochondriac. I knew I was sick, but after seeing doctor after doctor, the diagnosis never came. I would tell myself when I went to another specialist, "They're not going to find anything. Why am I even doing this anymore?" Every time I would go to the doctor, I would tell myself my blood pressure was going to be high, and, sure enough, it would be extremely elevated. I stopped eating. I stopped sleeping. I lost over sixty pounds, and I was making myself sicker than I already was. My family went on our yearly family vacations without me, and I was at home in bed.

In seeking answers, I asked myself the tough questions: Why is there so much suffering? Where is the justice for the oppressed? How can a loving God allow so much pain? These questions, once whispered in doubt, became a chorus of demand. Often, the response was silence. The heavens seemed indifferent, and the answers provided by religious authorities felt hollow. I began to wonder if I had been asking the wrong questions all along. I was ready to just throw in the towel and give up. What was left to do? I felt like I'd already tried every diet and every specialist out there. Was it long COVID, an autoimmune disease, or the ticks I'd found on me? There were so many possibilities. What was it? Was it all the medication I was on for high blood pressure, high cholesterol, indigestion, and many more? I was forty-five, and I had not one but two Monday-through-Friday pillboxes.

After years of anguish, I couldn't carry on. Doctors seemed clueless. Endless tests, empty results. So fed up with the relentless strain, I realized I needed a different approach.

I decided to take my health into my own hands. Instead of relying solely on doctors, I said to myself, "God, I want a refund." Right then, I began researching holistic remedies and alternative therapies.

I started re-experimenting with my diet, eliminating everything except clear liquids, incorporating natural supplements, and practicing mindfulness techniques. To my surprise, I began to notice small improvements in my health and well-being. Although progress was slow, it was a glimmer of hope I hadn't felt in years.

Empowered by these small victories, I continued my journey with renewed determination. I found solace in meditation, which helped me reconnect with my body and mind. I started journaling to track my symptoms and progress, finding patterns I hadn't noticed before.

I started talking with people with similar health struggles, gaining valuable insights and encouragement from their experiences. Over time, my outlook on life transformed. I felt more in control, more hopeful. I started seeing a new internal medicine doctor who was very well-known, and I slowly reintroduced one solid food at a time, eliminating them again if they caused any negative symptoms. Moving forward through positive affirmations, I learned to speak things that are not as though they were.

Be careful how you use your words and make sure that you don't use your words against yourself. Make sure you are not speaking those things like sickness into existence. Let me explain.

Maybe you say things like, "I don't want to be sick anymore. Please, I'm so sick and tired of being sick and tired. I just feel absolutely horrible every single day."

What you've just done is you've spoken through your mind, through your body, through your soul, through the cosmos, and straight to the creator that you want to be sick.

Listen to me when I say to speak things as though they are. Don't say things like, "I don't want to be sick anymore." You're just speaking sickness into existence and right into your life.

You're consuming yourself with the word "sick," and it's like sending an email out to a massive company. You just placed an order for sickness. All the buyers just got an order, and they sent shipments to your front door.

So listen closely. What we're going to do is say, "I am healthier than before. I am feeling better every day. I feel great. I feel amazing. Healing surrounds me. Thank you, thank you, thank you. I am so extremely grateful for all the healing in my life."

Next time you go to the doctor, think, "This is it. They are going to figure this out." Let those types of thoughts fill your mind. You have to think of the word "sick" as a dangerous word—so dangerous that every time you say it, it's like pouring gasoline right on a fire. Every time you say, "I'm so sick," you're pouring five gallons, fifty gallons, one hundred gallons of pure gasoline on a pile of old rotted wood.

Imagine you're standing within inches of that wood with a lighter in your hand, and you're about to bend down and light the fire. What's going to happen? I'll tell you exactly what's going to happen. It's going to explode in your face, and you're going to be injured and badly burned. You're going to get hurt. You're going to end up in the hospital or, even worse, dead. You have to think of that word, "sick," as if it is so dangerous that it will hurt you very badly. So never say that word again.

Try to think of other ways to explain. If you're going to a doctor and you just absolutely have to tell them that you're sick, say, "I'm just not feeling well" or "I'm feeling unwell." It is OK to explain to a physician that you're not feeling well, but that's it. You must tell yourself "I'm feeling well" every day, even if you don't. If you wake up exhausted and feeling beaten down, don't say to yourself, "This is going to be a long day." Instead, tell yourself, "I slept great last night, and I feel amazing. Today is going to be a great day." Stop telling yourself, "Mondays are the worst." Instead, tell yourself, "Mondays are great. I can't wait to get this week started."

All right, you got this. You see what I'm saying? Are you picking up what I'm putting down?

It's about sticking with positive reinforcement. Reframe your words because they shape your experience. Treat your words carefully. Words will create your reality, and negative words can spiral into physical harm. Take control of your words and your thoughts, and you'll take control of your life. Choose empowering language.

You have the power to transform your experiences by reframing how you express them. Remember, thoughts lead to feelings, and feelings lead to actions. It's the ripple effect: change your thoughts to change your life.

Say to yourself, "I get it. Words are powerful." Say it until you believe it. Practice daily until it becomes second nature. Remember, reframing negative thoughts with positive language can have a profound impact on your well-being. It's about creating a positive cycle through your words and thoughts. Seek out small wins each day. Celebrate them, no matter how minor. This act cements a positive mindset and builds momentum for a fulfilling, happy life.

Health is a multifaceted and dynamic concept that encompasses physical, mental, emotional, social, and environmental well-being. By understanding and nurturing each dimension, individuals can achieve a balanced and fulfilling life. The journey to optimal health is ongoing and requires commitment, self-awareness, and proactive measures. Embracing healthy habits and seeking support when needed can lead to a vibrant and resilient life.

For example, we absolutely have to change our typical American diet. It is literally killing us. We are slowly killing ourselves every day. Try to imagine that every time you eat things like hot dogs and potato chips, you are taking a day off your life. Just like debt, it adds up quickly. It's never too late to make a change.

I had always lived my life full of energy and on the go, but as I entered my forties, my health began to take an unexpected turn. My once-active lifestyle was replaced with more frequent visits to the doctor, and soon my medicine cabinet was filled with various prescriptions. I felt like I was living in a fog, each pill adding to my burden rather than alleviating it.

Determined to regain control over my health, I decided to take a different approach. I sought out a new doctor who was different from any doctor I had met before. She listened intently to my concerns and proposed a plan that focused on diet and lifestyle changes rather than just medication.

Under my new doctor and her amazing team's guidance, I began to overhaul my diet. Gone were the processed foods and sugary snacks that had become a staple in my daily routine. Instead, my meals were filled with fresh fruits, vegetables, and lean proteins. At first, the transition was challenging, but I soon discovered the joys of cooking and experimenting with new recipes. Each meal became an opportunity to nourish my body and mind.

In addition to dietary changes, Dr. A. P. and her team introduced me to a variety of sublingual supplements and encouraged me to incorporate regular exercise into my routine. I started with gentle activities like walking and meditation, gradually building up my strength and stamina. As the weeks passed, I noticed a significant improvement in my energy levels and overall well-being.

Slowly but surely, I began to reduce my prescription pill medications. With each visit, Dr. A. P. and her team would assess my progress and make adjustments as needed. It wasn't long before I was able to eliminate one medication after another. I was able to reduce my blood pressure meds and eliminate the cholesterol lowering medications like statins and fibrates I had been taking for years. My labs were once so bad that any numbers that were high or extremely elevated would show up in the color red. There was so much red that it looked like Jesus talking in the Bible. My triglycerides had been in the hundreds even with the medication but were now around fifty without them. The fog that had clouded my mind for so long seemed to lift, and I felt a renewed sense of clarity and purpose.

My journey to better health was not without its challenges, but the support of my new doctor and the changes I made to my lifestyle proved to be transformative. Today, I am proud to say that I am in the process of eliminating all of my medications. Through diet, exercise, and a holistic approach to wellness, including things like cold plunging, red light therapy, and earthing, I have taken control of my health and my life. Each day is a testament to the power of determination and the incredible impact of making mindful choices.

As the famous quote from *The Shawshank Redemption* says, "Get busy living, or get busy dying." Balancing health struggles with responsibilities is an immense challenge. I know firsthand how difficult it can be to push through days when you don't feel well, yet you still need to attend your kids' baseball and soccer games, fulfill your duties at work, and be present for your family. The weight of these responsibilities can feel overwhelming, but the desire not to miss those precious moments with your children drives you forward.

You find the strength within yourself because you know those moments are irreplaceable. Each game, each moment cheering from the sidelines, each hug and high five—they are the fabric of your children's memories and your own. Despite the fatigue and discomfort, you push through because giving up isn't an option. The love for your family and the commitment to your role as a parent and provider fuels your perseverance.

Remember, you are stronger than you realize. Even on the toughest days, you can do this. Keep going, not just for your loved ones but for yourself. Every step you take, every effort you make, is a testament to your resilience and dedication.

## Nutrition

A balanced diet rich in fruits, vegetables, whole grains, lean proteins, and healthy fats provides essential nutrients that support bodily functions. Avoiding excessive consumption of processed foods, sugar, and unhealthy fats can prevent chronic diseases such as obesity, diabetes, and heart disease.

## Food Sensitivities

These reactions are typically delayed and may not appear until several hours or even days after consuming the offending food. Common symptoms include digestive issues, headaches, fatigue, brain fog, and joint pain.

Try a food elimination diet plan that works for you. A food elimination diet is a structured approach used to identify food sensitivities, intolerances, or allergies by systematically removing and then reintroducing specific foods. This process helps individuals pinpoint which foods may be causing adverse reactions and subsequently make informed dietary choices to improve their health and well-being.

My diet consists of baked or grilled fish with a homemade lemon seasoning, black beans or black-eyed peas, low sodium turnip or collard greens, fresh fruit like apples, grapes, or blueberries, and vegetables.

## Exercise

Regular physical activity strengthens muscles, improves cardiovascular health, enhances flexibility, and boosts mental health. Adults should aim for at least 150 minutes of moderate-intensity aerobic activity or seventy-five minutes of vigorous-intensity activity per week, along with muscle-strengthening exercises on two or more days a week.

## Sleep

Quality sleep is vital for physical and mental restoration. Adults typically need seven to nine hours of sleep per night. Good sleep practices, such as maintaining a regular sleep schedule, creating a restful environment, and avoiding stimulants before bedtime, can improve sleep quality.

## Preventive Health Care

Regular checkups, screenings, and healthy lifestyle choices can prevent or detect health issues early. Preventive measures such as maintaining a healthy weight, managing stress, and avoiding smoking and excessive alcohol consumption are crucial.

Turning inward, I found that the search for God was really a search for meaning within myself. Spirituality became a personal journey rather than a prescribed set of rules. I found solace in the understanding that faith is not about answers but about the journey itself. The idea of demanding a refund from God transformed into an acceptance of the complexities of existence. In seeking a refund from God, I found not an end but a new beginning—an ever-evolving relationship with the divine, grounded in the realities of life and the depths of the human heart.

1. The next time you have a new doctor's appointment, tell yourself, "They are going to figure this out. I can feel it in my bones."

2. Tell yourself that you are better every day. When someone asks you how you are feeling, you will say, "With my hands." Then laugh and say, "Better every day."

3. Envision yourself doing something you love. Close your eyes and picture yourself in your happy place.
4. Speak things into existence by speaking positive thoughts and words into your life.
5. When it comes to your health, stay off of Google!
6. Say, "GOD, I want a refund from all the times I've let not feeling well hold me back from living live to the fullest."

"Healing yourself is connected with healing others."
—*Yoko Ono*

# CHAPTER 2
## STOP FORCING OUR BELIEFS ON OTHERS

The diversity of human thought is as vast and varied as the people who inhabit this planet. Each person carries a unique set of experiences, cultures, and perspectives that shape their beliefs and values. Yet throughout history, there has been a persistent tendency among individuals and groups to impose their beliefs on others.

I am a Christian, and I believe in God in the form of Jesus Christ, Lord and Savior. If you are a Christian, then you believe that with all your heart and soul. If you are a Buddhist or into Hinduism, that's your choice. Hinduism is one of the oldest religions on this planet; who are we to judge them?

This might upset a few people. This is not what this is meant to do; this is meant for us to be free and love one another. Lift each other up. Take a deep breath and send out positive thoughts and positive prayers. Why do you think people say, "Our thoughts and prayers are with you"? It comes from the very beginning of time. Our thoughts are so powerful. We must respect everyone's journey and allow them to find their own path. Life's challenges can be overwhelming, but it is essential to focus on what we can control.

Beliefs are deeply personal. They are often rooted in cultural, religious, or personal experiences and can be fundamental to an individual's identity. When someone attempts to force their beliefs on others, it can feel like an attack on their very being. This can lead to resistance, resentment, and a breakdown in communication.

## The Right to Individual Beliefs

Every person has the right to hold their own beliefs. This right is enshrined in various human rights charters and constitutions around the world. Take care of your mental well-being and embrace kindness and compassion. There have been so many wars and so many lives lost over forced religion. It's important to acknowledge and respect the diverse beliefs and experiences of others and focus on unity and love regardless of our differences.

Why can't we come together and talk about religion or politics? I will tell you why. Because someone will get upset or someone else will be offended. Just try to imagine a world where we could come together from all religions. Go outside, breathe some fresh air, and remember that your strength comes from within. I understand your frustration. However, it's important to focus on what truly matters. A small amount of kindness goes a long way. Take a deep breath and stop worrying so much; your journey will be fine. Finding peace within yourself is paramount. Focus on empathy, love, and understanding in your interactions.

Embrace the small moments of joy and recognize the beauty around you.

We can be whoever we choose to be in life. We can say, "God, I want a refund." Just like in a card game, if you don't like the cards that are in front of you at the moment, that's OK. Then guess what? There's a whole new set coming around next hand. It's OK to say, "I don't like this hand. I'm going to fold this round." But you wouldn't tell everyone at the table, "I'm folding, and y'all should fold also." The person across from you might think, "I'm holding pocket aces. I'm not folding." All I'm saying is you can be whoever or whatever you choose; just don't force it on others around you. Life's a card game. Sometimes it's a gamble. Play your hand the best you can and remember that each new round offers new opportunities. Take control of your circumstances as best you can. Focus on your growth and resilience. In life's game, learning from every round is key to improving your strategy.

The first step toward avoiding the imposition of beliefs is cultivating empathy and open-mindedness. Empathy allows us to understand

and share the feelings of others, while open-mindedness enables us to consider different perspectives without immediate judgment. Together, these qualities foster an environment of mutual respect and understanding.

Politics—oh boy, let me walk on some eggshells here. It's sad that the conversation of politics will upset others more than a conversation about God, our Creator. When it comes to politics, we get so passionate about our beliefs and how we believe daily operations should run or how money should be spent.

As I sit here writing this, the news blares in the background, a stark reminder of the turbulent times we live in. The anchor's voice is tinged with urgency and disbelief as she reports an assassination attempt on former-President Trump. The gravity of the situation sends a chill down my spine, and I pause, my fingers hovering over the keyboard, struggling to process the enormity of what has just happened.

My thoughts drift to the deep-seated anger and division that have gripped our country and the escalating political divisions that have pitted neighbor against neighbor, friend against friend.

The news continues to unfold, detailing how a gunman, driven by extreme hatred toward someone they had never even met, infiltrated the rally, weapon in hand, ready to take a life in the name of his beliefs. Why? Because his views are different than yours? It's a stark reminder of how far we've fallen, how the discourse has deteriorated into violence and vitriol.

My mind races back to a simpler time when disagreements were settled with words, not weapons. When we could debate, argue, and still find common ground at the end of the day. But now, it seems, we've lost that ability. The lines are drawn so sharply, the sides so divided, that violence feels like the only option for some.

I think of the families torn apart by politics, the friendships strained by differing views, and the communities fractured by the endless cycle of blame and anger. The attempted assassination is not just an attack on a man but on the very fabric of our democracy, the principles that bind us together as a nation.

As I sit here, I think to myself, "The violence and hatred have to stop. We need to find a way to bridge the divide, to remember our shared humanity. We must reject the narrative that paints our opponents as enemies and instead seek to understand their fears and concerns."

The screen flashes with images of the aftermath and the brave souls who rushed to aid the wounded. It's a reminder that even in the darkest of times, there is still hope, still compassion, still a glimmer of the goodness that defines us.

I turn back to my writing, determined to use my words as a beacon of light in these dark times. We must stand together, reject the hatred, and work toward a future where such acts of violence are a distant memory. The road ahead is long and arduous, but it's a journey we must undertake for the sake of our children, our country, and our collective future.

The violence and hatred have to stop. And it starts with each of us, right here, right now.

No matter what side of the fence you're on, you have to move forward and remember one thing when it comes to politics: the left wing and the right wing both belong to the same bird. If you were to cut the left wing off, the bird would fly in circles and not ever be able to get off the ground. If you cut the right wing off also, you will eventually kill the bird. A bird needs both its wings to survive.

When the debates get heated, we must seek balance for the greater good. Understanding this helps foster more productivity for working people. So let's find common ground—solutions that support the well-being of all. We have to learn to work together again. Mutual respect and empathy could mend the division, guiding us toward a more harmonious society. Real progress lies in cooperation, setting aside differences for a stronger, united future.

How many of us look at the outside appearance of others and think to ourselves, "Wow, there's no way I would ever walk outside looking like that"? We have to learn to accept others for who they are or who they want to be. When we pass each other on the street, we look at each other as though we are from different worlds, but in reality, if you were to sit down and have a cup of coffee with that person, you would be amazed at how much you really have in common.

Each of us carries a unique story, a tapestry of experiences. And when we judge based on appearance, we miss the essence of these stories. Appearances can be deceptive, masking the true character of a person.

When I was younger—in my early twenties—I just knew I was going to be a rock star one day, and I dressed just like that. But I had also been raised as a country boy with cowboy boots and a cowboy hat, so I would walk on stage in downtown Memphis, Tennessee, playing rock music with the cowboy hat on. My music career and playing shows was definitely an experience. I will always cherish those memories, but that's another story for another time.

Fast forward to later in life. I sometimes wear a cowboy hat to work and have for years. I have never forced that on anyone. One day, I came in and noticed that a large group of the guys I work with were all wearing cowboy hats. I laughed, and I said, "See? The hat blocks the sun and shades your head on those extremely hot sunny days, doesn't it?" Guys who had previously told me, "You will never catch me in a cowboy hat" were now wearing cowboy hats. One guy even posted videos of himself playing "Free Bird" online. My point here is to never force things on others. Just live your life. I still have others who work with me who tell me, "You will never catch me in a cowboy hat." And you know what? That's fine. I don't expect them to try it out. Everyone has their own path and preferences, and that's OK. I'll enjoy the shade it brings.

Parents, now this is going to be a very large pill for you to swallow. Don't force the things you love and are extremely passionate about on your children. I can recall that when my first son was born, I told my wife, "I'm going to go down to the local music store here in town and buy him a brand new Gibson Les Paul from the year he was born."

My father had a 1978 Les Paul guitar from the year I was born. I would give anything to know where that guitar is and bring it back home to our family. My dream was to do the same for my son—but to preserve this one so he could have it one day, driven by my passion for finding the guitar my father had sold for drugs.

One day, my wife looked at me and said, "Honey, what if he doesn't want to play the guitar like you?" At the time, I thought, "Oh, he's going to play the guitar." But over time, I realized my wife was right. We can't impose our passions on our children. They should be free to find their own interests and paths.

It's important to let our children explore their own passions. So many parents force their children to play sports, play an instrument, or follow a specific career path because they themselves love these things or have unfulfilled dreams. Everyone needs the chance to carve out their own identity, especially our children.

It's like a new mother not understanding why her baby won't eat. Perhaps she constantly calls the physician, takes the baby to the doctor, and worries, saying things like, "My baby won't latch. I've tried every formula, and the baby won't eat. I don't know what I'm going to do." The doctor will ask her to sit down and be calm, reassuring her that the baby will eat when they're hungry—they're not going to starve to death. A small amount of the mother's milk goes a long way. After taking a deep breath and not worrying so much, she can trust that her baby will be fine.

In the same way, we should trust our children to find their own way, to eat when they're hungry, and to pursue their passions when they're ready. We can guide and support them, but ultimately they need the freedom to discover who they are and what they love on their own terms.

The imposition of beliefs is not only harmful but also counterproductive. It breeds division, stifles growth, and causes psychological harm. By fostering empathy, engaging in respectful dialogue, encouraging critical thinking, and recognizing common ground, we can create a more harmonious and inclusive society. The diversity of human thought should be celebrated, not suppressed. By respecting each other's beliefs, we contribute to a world where everyone has the freedom to be themselves.

1.  Remember to let go and let God
2.  Remember to say, "Only God can judge me."
3.  Remember the left wing and right wing belong to the same bird.
4.  Remember everyone has their own path and preferences, and that's OK.
5.  Do not impose your passions on others. They should be free to find their own interests and paths.
6.  Remember to say "God, I want a refund" from a world filled with so much hate. Jesus never said, "Go force people to believe." He said to them,

"Go into all the world and *preach the gospel* to all creation"
(Mark 16:15, emphasis mine).

# CHAPTER 3
# **ADDICTION**

Addiction can come in many forms: sex, drugs, gambling, overeating, television, internet, smartphones or tablets, and more. It's a chronic condition that can affect many aspects of your life, including your physical and mental health, relationships, and career. With proper treatment and self-care, people break the addiction cycle all the time. Knowing when to seek help is crucial when it feels overwhelming. Remember, you're not alone.

While I was growing up, both of my parents battled addiction. My father was addicted to crack cocaine, and my mother struggled with alcohol and pills. They always found excuses to use. I remember my father telling my mother one day, "A bee could die outside, and you would have an excuse to drink." Later in life, I still recall him saying, "Let me guess, the bee died." The irony, of course, was that they both had their own struggles, using any minor stressor as a reason to use their drug of choice. This became a never-ending cycle that went on for years.

Looking back, it's no wonder their constant relapses left such a deep impression on me. I remember sharing a gas station Twinkie with my father, bought with change we found under the couch cushions in our trailer. We put a candle in it, and he sang "Happy Birthday" to me. There were no gifts to open, just me and him sharing one Twinkie, and I was grateful for the memory. It wasn't until years later that I truly understood the weight of those moments.

Eventually, my parents became absent, and at twelve years old, I stopped going to school, ending up with a fifth-grade education. There were times when I would come home to find the lights off and no food in our house. I remember eating cinnamon toast folded in half three times a day. That's probably why I can't eat cinnamon toast anymore. I remember watching a commercial on television about drugs and the person losing their job, house, money, and family. I thought, "How do you lose your family?" It wasn't until my parents separated due to their addictions that I understood.

My parents' addictions tore us apart. But despite everything, there was a part of me that still hoped for a better ending. That hope, fragile as it was, kept me moving forward. I learned to ask God for a refund.

Most of us have found ourselves glued to our phones. Put your phone down and look around—you'll see everyone is on their phones constantly. The world has become a place where real connections are often overshadowed by virtual interactions. We are so consumed with screens that we miss out on the world right in front of us. It troubles me to think about what we're losing: the simple joys of human interaction, the spontaneous conversations, and the sense of community. Our children have no idea how to communicate without their phones. This generation has become so socially reclusive and disconnected from reality. I find myself wondering if we can ever reverse this trend.

How can we reclaim genuine connections in a world dominated by screens? I'll tell you how. Try putting your phone down and talking to the people right in front of you. Go outside, take a walk, look at nature, and start interacting with the people around you. Talk to the people you work with over a cup of coffee in the morning. You might learn they are going through something and really need someone to talk to—or just someone to listen, not just pretend to listen while looking at their phone. Go to lunch with an old friend and don't look at your phone unless there's an emergency. Spend time with family without the distraction of screens—play a game, cook a meal and sit down at the dining room table together, or simply have a long conversation. When you get home, start with "How was your day today?" and really pay attention to what they are telling you.

When I worked at Elvis Presley's Graceland, I remember going to lunch every Friday at the Catfish Cabin with Vester Presley, Elvis Presley's uncle. Elvis's cousin, Jimmy, and I would listen to him tell stories about Elvis and Graceland. I can still remember those stories like it was yesterday because we didn't have cell phones back then. You could just enjoy a nice meal and listen to the conversations of others around you. I'll get more into stories from my five years at Graceland later on.

I had a family member tell me that they just can't do AA meetings because it reminds them of how badly they want a drink. Now don't get me wrong—AA meetings have worked for so many people, and I would never say don't go, but if you have a loved one who says the meetings are a reminder of how badly they want a drink, listen to them and try a different approach. I can only imagine having an addiction to something and someone telling me one day that I could never have that again. What if someone told you one day that you could never have your favorite food ever again, and then they wanted you to attend meetings that talked about that food for an hour straight? All I'm saying is listen to them and ask questions about what steps would work best for them. Be supportive by exploring other recovery options that might be more fitting for your loved one.

"Take the first step in faith. You don't have to see the whole staircase, just take the first step."
—Dr. Martin Luther King, Jr.

The absolute worst thing you can do is be a crutch for someone who is battling addiction by enabling them. You have to set boundaries and stick by your decision. Encourage them to find healthy coping mechanisms and don't enable their destructive habits. Remember, it's important to show empathy and understanding without compromising your own well-being or enabling harmful behaviors. I can remember all the countless hours I've spent worrying and wondering if I made the right decisions, stressing over whether I was too tough on someone this time. Was I being too hard on them, or was I not pushing hard enough? You have to stand by your decisions and never back down. It's no different than if you grounded one of your children for doing something wrong and then you turned right around and said, "Never mind, you're not grounded anymore." They would never learn from their mistakes. And everyone has to be on the same page. Don't be an enabler. If my wife grounded one of our kids, I wouldn't turn right around and let them off the hook. Set boundaries and stand together, no matter how tough it seems or how painful the decision was to make. That decision just might save their lives. So hold fast to your principles and believe that the decisions you've made will lead to clarity and healing.

1. Don't try to do this alone. Please never be afraid to ask for help.
2. Stop using stress as an excuse to use. Stop lying to yourself and others.
3. Listen and be supportive. Be open-minded to the struggles of others.
4. Don't be a crutch by enabling someone. Let me say that again for the people in the back: do not be a crutch by enabling them.
5. Put your devices down and walk away. Try to enjoy what's actually going on all around you. And never give up.
6. "God, I want a refund from believing that I can fix everything on my own. This isn't just about them—it's about my own growth too."

"Nobody is gonna hit as hard as life. But it ain't about how hard you hit. It's about how hard you can get hit and keep moving forward; how much you can take and keep moving forward. That's how winning is done!"
—*Rocky Balboa*

# CHAPTER 4
# STOP BLAMING OTHERS

Stop playing the blame game. We love to blame others for our own problems. You wouldn't blame a spoon for making you overeat, would you? So why are you blaming others for your faults? Take responsibility for your own actions.

Have you ever found yourself blaming your spouse for a particular situation or problem? Do you ever find yourself asking, "Why are you always complaining about the laundry?" The response is always "You can start doing the laundry yourself. I bet you don't even know how the washing machine works. Heck, you probably don't even know where the laundry room is, do you?" In the voice of Scooby-Doo, "Rut-ro." That didn't end well, did it? Now you are in a full-blown argument. Are the kids listening? I'll get more into this in the relationships chapter, but you get my point.

Have you ever blamed someone else for your bad day at work? For example, you come home from a long day, and the first wrong thing your spouse or kids say, you bite their heads off. It's unfair to unload your frustrations on them. They had nothing to do with your rough day. That's why it is so important to start every day with positive thoughts like "Today is going to be a great day. Nothing and no one can put me in a bad mood, no matter the situation." Taking ownership of your emotions is crucial. How you handle stress can significantly impact your relationships.

Taking responsibility also means learning to understand and regulate your emotions. How many times have you been in traffic and the driver in front of you is either not paying attention or lost? You are already running late, so you get angry, start blowing the horn, and throw your hands up. You pull up next to them and start yelling from your window. Next thing you know, you find yourself in an all-out road rage situation. Whose fault is that? The person who only took a few seconds away from you? Or you, for making yourself late? Let me help you out: it's you. It's you because you are responsible for how you react to situations.

Reflect on how you could handle such situations differently. Ask yourself, "How could I have handled that situation better?" Reflect on the triggers that prompt such intense reactions. Find ways to manage your frustrations effectively. Practice patience and embrace techniques that calm your mind. When you get frustrated with a situation or conversation, try to calm yourself by asking how you would feel if someone were talking to your mother or child the way you just did to that person. We have to stop treating people badly and blaming others for our own mistakes. People will not remember what triggered you, just how you reacted.

Take responsibility for your actions and the impact they have on others. Learn to swallow your pride and say, "I'm sorry."

Have you ever walked into a room to find two children arguing and then noticed something has been broken? You ask both of them, "Who did it?" They both point at each other and respond with, "They did it." If you are a parent of more than one child, you know the answer is yes. They are so afraid of being in trouble or getting grounded that they are willing to throw their own sibling under the bus for something they've done. How many parents have just walked away and said, "Well then, you're both grounded since no one wants to tell the truth"? In many circumstances, that will work just fine, but it doesn't address the fact that one of them just blamed the other.

Accountability is crucial for personal growth. By addressing our actions and admitting when we're wrong, we encourage honesty and integrity within ourselves and others. So try a little reverse psychology. Try telling them, "OK, no one will be in trouble if whoever did it just tells me the truth. If I find out this was just an accident and you didn't mean to do it, then you'll both be let off the hook." This approach can sometimes prompt the admission you're looking for since the fear of punishment is removed. You still have to address the fact that one of them blamed the other, and you have to let them know that this is not OK and that you are very disappointed in them for this. Instilling honesty in children requires patience and balanced consequences.

I learned these principles later on in life, after working many different jobs and being fired for making minor mistakes like not putting the seatbelt on every time I got on and off a forklift. I was so afraid of telling the truth because I was afraid of losing my job. I would be so consumed with thoughts like, "How am I going to pay my mortgage? How am I going to put gas in my vehicle? How am I going to put groceries in the refrigerator?" Now that I'm in a supervisor position, I always try to imagine myself in their situation. And I tell them, "Just tell me what happened, and you are not going to lose your job. We will just document this and move on. We need you just as much as you need this job." This empathy-driven approach helps create a supportive work environment.

Stop blaming others for you not succeeding in life. Do you know how easy it would have been for me to blame my parents and my upbringing for every circumstance that didn't go my way in my life?

Blame is an instinctive reaction. When things go wrong, our first impulse is often to identify a culprit, point a finger, and offload responsibility. This tendency, while deeply rooted in human nature, is counterproductive in personal relationships, professional environments, and even within ourselves. We need to look at the underlying reasons for its prevalence and effective strategies to shift from a culture of blame to one of accountability and growth.

Blame disrupts trust and cooperation. In any setting, whether it's at home, at work, or within social groups, assigning blame creates an atmosphere of fear and defensiveness. When individuals feel they are at risk of being blamed, they are less likely to take risks, admit mistakes, or collaborate openly. This leads to a stifling environment where innovation and progress are hindered.

In professional settings, blame can cause a toxic culture. Employees may become more focused on self-preservation than on the collective goals of the organization. Blame can lead to resentment, reduced morale, and high turnover rates. It creates division within departments or teams unwilling to share information or resources, fearing the repercussions of failure.

On a personal level, blame can destroy relationships. When partners or family members blame each other, it often leads to cycles of conflict and defensiveness. Blame overshadows understanding and empathy, preventing meaningful resolution of issues. Over time, it can cause lasting damage to the emotional bonds between people.

1. Stop blaming others for your actions.
2. Ask yourself, "How could I have handled that situation better?"
3. Take responsibility for your actions and the impacts they have on others.
4. Put yourself in others' shoes and try to think how your actions will affect others.
5. Swallow your pride. Be humble and honest with yourself.
6. Say "God, I want a refund" every time you've been blamed for someone else's actions—and anytime you are tempted to avoid acknowledging your own faults and responsibilities.

"You can't blame gravity for falling in love."
—*Albert Einstein*

# CHAPTER 5
# NEVER GIVE UP ON YOUR HOPES AND DREAMS

You can never move forward if you're always looking backward. You are in a place in your life right now that tells you where you are, with all the battles and struggles you've been through. All of the things that made you who you are today and all the things that you've overcome in your life are molding the person you are going to become in life. Trust in that process because every step you take is building a stronger foundation for your future. We've been told our entire lives, "Don't try to walk before you can crawl." Forget that—I say let's all take off running and chase our dreams with pure passion, emotion, and determination, for only then will we truly soar.

We all have dreams and goals we would love to achieve. So why don't we go after them? I'll tell you why. Because we either get stuck in a rut or we let fear hold us back. We create excuses, and doubt starts to creep in, whispering lies that we aren't good enough or capable enough. We find ourselves saying, "I can't do that." Well...why not? Why not indeed? There's nothing stopping us, just the barriers we build in our minds. Don't let those barriers define you. Break through them with courage, faith, and a relentless spirit. No one ever achieved greatness by sitting on the sidelines.

"You miss 100 percent of the shots you don't take."
—Wayne Gretzky

This Wayne Gretzky quote was on a six-foot-tall dry-erase board in my house. It belonged to my father-in-law. He would tell his sales associates this during his meetings. I ended up with it and would look at it every day for a long time. I knew I wanted to do something one day. Maybe I would start my own business or play music, but I never imagined writing a book would ever be in the realm of possibilities. Remember, I have only completed the fifth grade. Thanks to my wife pushing me, I did go back and acquire a GED. Life can sometimes take unexpected turns, presenting you with opportunities you never considered before. Don't be afraid to take a chance and seize those moments. Pursuing a path outside your comfort zone can lead to incredible personal growth and unexpected achievements.

What if I told you that I always knew I was destined to be a rock star? Growing up, I dreamed of electric guitars, roaring crowds, and the thrill of performing under the bright lights. My dad's 1978 Les Paul guitar in my hands, I spent countless hours perfecting my craft, convinced that one day I would make something of myself.

In the heart of Memphis, where the legacy of blues and rock 'n' roll runs deep, there was a band called Shameface. Comprised of Robert, Jason, Travis, Anthony, and Zane, they were a tight-knit group brought together by a shared love of music and a dream of making it big. We practiced in my garage, our sound a blend of raw energy and heartfelt lyrics driven by powerful melodic guitar riffs and a tight rhythm section.

Shameface quickly gained a reputation in the local music scene, our shows becoming a magnet for music lovers. We played every venue we could find, from the new daisy, the Hard Rock Café, to outdoor festivals, our passion evident in every performance. We played shows with Egypt Central, Rail, Piston Honda, Muck Sticky, In the Balance, Logic 34, Crippled Nation, and so many more.

Our first show together was at a packed venue in downtown Memphis. The air was electric with anticipation. The band took the stage, and the crowd erupted in applause. We launched into our first song, the powerful sound of the guitars echoing through the venue. Travis's vocals soared, backed by solid bass lines and intricate drumming. The chemistry between us was palpable, and the audience could feel it. We went on to play show after show from Memphis to New Orleans and everywhere in between.

But life, with its unpredictable twists and turns, had other plans for me. The path to stardom wasn't as straightforward as I had imagined. Instead of stadium tours and platinum records, I found myself writing songs and channeling my passion into crafting songs that others would one day bring to life. At first, it felt like a detour, a compromise. But as the years went by, I began to see it differently.

I started my own home music studio, a modest setup that gradually grew into a nice space where creativity thrived. My studio became a haven for aspiring musicians. I found joy in helping them discover their sound, recording their music, and watching their stories take flight. I realized that my studio wasn't about my own achievements; it was also about the impact I could have on others.

One of my proudest moments came when the chief of police, a man named Pirtle, approached me with an unusual request. He and his wife, Jamie, had formed a gospel group called Entering Heaven, and they wanted to record an album. They had heard about my studio and my work, and they believed I could help bring their vision to life.

Recording that gospel album was a transformative experience. Pirtle and Jamie poured their hearts into every song, their voices filled with faith and hope. As I worked with them, I felt a deep connection to the music, a sense of purpose that transcended my initial dreams of rock stardom. The album was a testament to their devotion, and when it was finally complete, the joy and gratitude in their eyes were worth more than any applause I could have received on stage.

Life has a way of surprising you with opportunities you never saw coming. While I didn't become the rock star I once envisioned, I found something even more meaningful. I discovered the power of music to uplift, inspire, and transform lives. I learned that my true calling wasn't just to perform but to help others succeed, to be a part of their journey and watch them shine.

Looking back, I wouldn't change a thing. Every twist and turn, every unexpected possibility, led me to where I am today. My home music studio became more than just a place to record songs; it became a beacon of creativity and collaboration, a space where dreams were nurtured and brought to life. And in helping others achieve their dreams, I found a fulfillment that surpassed my wildest rock star fantasies.

So what if I told you that life doesn't always go as planned? Sometimes, it leads you to places you never imagined, presenting you with opportunities to make a difference in ways you never anticipated. Embrace the surprises, cherish the journey, and remember that success isn't just about reaching the top; it's also about the lives you touch along the way.

Did you know that nine recording studios passed on the band Lynyrd Skynyrd—and that was after hearing "Free Bird"? They all said it was way too long and would never get a second of airtime. Now that song is one of the most requested songs of all time. They also said "Simple Man" had no meaning, and they asked the band to scrap that song. Ronnie Van Zant took the executive producer out to his car, rolled the window down, shut the door, and said, "We will call you when we're done recording 'Simple Man.'" Never give up on your dreams.

With the help of my neighbor—let's call him Dave—I had embarked on an ambitious project: building guitars from scratch. I was able to get the wood from cherry and black walnut trees that had been removed to make way for future development at Silo Square in Southaven, Mississippi. The process was long and tiring but deeply satisfying. Each piece of wood was carefully cut, sanded, and shaped with precision. One of the guitars, crafted in the shape of a one-of-a-kind Native American arrowhead, became a particular point of pride. The design was unique, and the craftsmanship was evident in every curve and detail. When it was finally assembled, the guitar played beautifully, its sound rich and resonant.

These guitars were more than just instruments; they were works of art born from perseverance and passion. They now hang in the Lucky Dog restaurant at Silo Square, where you can go see them today. People text me pictures of the guitars all the time, asking me the story behind them.

I also built a custom bass guitar for Pierre Wells, the former bass player of the North Mississippi Allstars.

Looking at those guitars, I couldn't help but reflect on my journey. There had been times when I felt like giving up, times when the challenges seemed insurmountable. But I had pushed through, driven by a belief that I could achieve something extraordinary. Standing in the restaurant, watching people admire our work, I felt a profound sense of accomplishment.

My message to anyone who will listen is clear: "Yes, you can." Life is full of unexpected paths and hidden possibilities. Sometimes, the road less traveled leads to the most rewarding destinations. The guitars were a testament to that truth, a reminder that with determination and a bit of creativity, anything is possible.

The journey of building those guitars taught me that success isn't always about following a straightforward path. It's about embracing challenges, finding new ways to express your passions, and never giving up on your dreams. And sometimes, with a little help from a good neighbor, you can create something truly remarkable.

"All our dreams can come true if we have the courage to pursue them."
—*Walt Disney*

Looking around at all the new developments in Southaven and the neighboring cities and counties, I'm struck by the realization that each building, park, and roadway started with a simple thought. Every piece of progress we see around us was once just an idea in someone's mind. The shopping centers, thriving businesses, and expanding neighborhoods—all of these began as mere concepts.

The difference between an idea and the tangible reality we now witness is action. Those who conceived these developments didn't just let their thoughts drift away; they acted on them, turning their visions into plans and then into physical structures. They faced challenges, made sacrifices, and persisted until their dreams materialized.

It's a powerful reminder that every great achievement starts with a single thought. It inspires me to believe in the power of my own ideas and to take the necessary steps to bring them to life. The transformation of our surroundings shows that with dedication and effort, even the simplest thought can grow into something remarkable.

1. Never give up on your dreams.
2. Don't be afraid to try new things.
3. Never say "I can't do that" because can't never could.
4. Stay positive and take chances.
5. Step outside of your comfort zone and make it happen.
6. Say "God, I want a refund" for every time someone tells you, "You can't do that."

"You may say I'm a dreamer, but I'm not the only one."
—*John Lennon*

# CHAPTER 6
# THE ANSWER IS ALWAYS NO IF YOU DON'T ASK

I've been employed for over twenty years in the thriving city of South-aven, Mississippi. I work for the city's utility department. My days are filled with overseeing water and sewer systems, ensuring the lifelines of the city function seamlessly. We all take immense pride in our work, but often I find myself contemplating ways to improve the efficiency and effectiveness of the utility department.

One pressing issue that generated frequent complaints was the con-stant damage of the city residents' sewer lines. Traditional repair meth-ods were time-consuming and often led to unexpected problems that were costly to fix. I believed there was a better way—using advanced camera technology to inspect the sewer lines proactively. Identifying potential issues before and after contractors installed utilities would help the customers find any major problems before they ended up costing thousands of dollars' worth of damage from backed-up sewer lines.

Over several months, I researched and gathered information about various camera systems and the contractors who could implement this technology. I compiled data, case studies from other cities, and cost-benefit analyses, crafting a comprehensive proposal. However, I was battling with how I would present this idea to the city's leadership, particularly the mayor.

One afternoon, my director, Mr. Ray Humphrey, said, "Robert, you've been deep in thought lately. What's on your mind?"

Taking a breath, I explained my idea. Director Humphrey listened intently, nodding with interest. "This sounds like a game changer, Robert. Why haven't you presented it to the mayor yet?"

I hesitated. "I guess I'm worried it might not be well received. It's a significant change and would cost thousands of dollars. I'm not sure if the mayor will go for it."

Mr. Humphrey smiled kindly. "Robert, if anyone can pull this off and talk them into it, it's you. You've done your homework. You believe in this idea, and it's clear it could benefit our city greatly. The mayor needs to hear it."

Encouraged by his words, I decided it was time to take the leap. We scheduled a meeting with the mayor, Mr. Musselwhite, who was known for his openness to innovation but also for his rigorous scrutiny of new proposals.

On the day of the meeting, we walked into the mayor's office with a mixture of nerves and determination. Mayor Musselwhite greeted us warmly. "Robert, Mr. Humphrey tells me you have an interesting proposal for us. I'd love to hear it."

I launched into my presentation, outlining the benefits of using camera technology for sewer inspections before and after contractors and boring companies installed their fiber optic cables. I detailed how this proactive approach could save the city money, reduce emergency repairs, and improve overall efficiency.

As I spoke, I noticed the mayor's interest growing. When I finished, there was a brief silence. Mayor Musselwhite leaned back in his chair, contemplating the information.

"Robert," he began, "this is an impressive proposal. The thoroughness of your research is commendable. Implementing this could indeed help prevent citizens from being responsible for the contractors' mistakes. This will save our citizens thousands on sewer repairs. I'm convinced. Let's move forward with this idea to test its feasibility in our city."

Relief and elation surged through me. The mayor's approval was a significant step forward, and it validated all the hard work we had put into the proposal.

Over the next few months, my idea was implemented. Contractors equipped with state-of-the-art cameras began inspecting the sewer lines before and after work had been completed, and the results were even better than anticipated. Potential issues were identified and addressed before they escalated, saving the city and our citizens substantial amounts of money and minimizing disruptions to residents.

I started getting phone calls and emails from other municipalities in the neighboring cities and counties saying, "Wow. What are y'all doing? Because it's working."

The success of this program led to a full-scale implementation of the technology across Southaven. The initiative not only improved the efficiency of the utility department, but it also stopped many complaints.

Reflecting on the journey, I often shared my experience with colleagues: "Remember, the answer is always no if you don't ask. Don't let fear hold you back from presenting your ideas. Sometimes, all it takes is that one question to bring about meaningful change."

This story became an inspiring example within the city, encouraging others to voice their ideas and take bold steps toward improvement. In the heart of Southaven, this was a testament to the power of asking and the transformative impact it could have on the community.

In any aspect of your life, whether it's with your job, goals you have, asking God for a refund, or your relationship (single or married), you can implement the idea of telling yourself, "The answer is always no if you don't ask." Think about that for just a second. You will always be single and never get married, settle down, and have that family you've always dreamed about if you never ask that person out. Why are you so nervous? Just walk over and introduce yourself. What's the worst that will happen? They say no. I'll say it again: "The answer is always no if you don't ask."

Your hesitation isn't unique to you. Throughout your life, maybe you've often held back from asking for what you wanted, whether it was a promotion, a date, or even a favor from a friend. The fear of hearing "no" was a constant barrier, preventing you from taking risks and seizing opportunities.

Be determined to change your pattern. Decide to take a step forward. Open that laptop and send that email. Hit send before you can second-guess yourself. You'll feel a rush of adrenaline. The fishing line has been cast out, and there is no turning back. Now sit back and wait for the biggest opportunities of your life.

1. Don't be afraid to ask for what you truly want in life.
2. Don't be afraid of the word "no." It's just a word.
3. Don't be afraid to take chances. If you believe in something, then go after it.
4. Believe in yourself and run after your dreams.
5. Stay determined and don't hesitate to ask. Remember, the answer is always no if you don't ask.
6. Say "God, I want a refund" for every time I've hesitated to ask and missed another opportunity.

"We will fail when we fail to try."
—Rosa Parks

# CHAPTER 7
# MANAGING EVERYDAY STRUGGLES

I can remember when I was a child and my parents brought out a can of beans for us to split for dinner. And later as a teenager, I remember taking a slice of bread and putting it in the toaster oven covered in cinnamon, butter, and sugar. I would fold that one slice in half, and that would be my meal for the day. These memories highlight the challenges of living with limited resources and the impact such experiences can have on one's emotional and mental well-being. That's probably why sometimes I tend to overbuy things for my children.

I know what it's like to struggle and go without. I've been there. At one point in my life, my father was homeless and living in a shelter on Third Street in Memphis, Tennessee, and my mother was struggling to take care of herself. She couldn't afford to take care of both of us. So I lived with my grandmother until she passed away from cancer.

My wife and I met while working at Elvis Presley's Graceland. She was a tour guide, and I was on the maintenance crew. I struggled to pay my bills, living paycheck to paycheck. Only by doing side jobs and working day and night seven days a week was I barely able to make ends meet. When we had our first child, I vowed to give him a life better than I ever had. Through years of tireless work and dedication, together with the help of others who believed in us, we managed to make an amazing life for our family. Now, years later, I look back at those tough times and remind myself why it's so important not to take anything for granted.

And no matter what life throws at you, keep moving forward and never give up.

Growing up, I can remember thinking how much I wished I had Sheetrock on my walls—something solid, something I could paint. In those days, it was hard to imagine a life beyond the immediate struggles. Yet as I look around now, I'm filled with gratitude and amazement at how far I've come.

I never would have imagined that I would have such an amazing family. I have a beautiful, loving, and caring wife, Natalie, who stands by me through thick and thin. Our two amazing, perfectly healthy children bring joy and laughter into our lives every day. Their smiles and achievements are constant reminders of the blessings we've received.

Adding to this, I have a mother and father-in-law who love me like their own. Their support and acceptance have been invaluable, creating a sense of belonging and family unity that I cherish deeply. Thank you, Lynn and Fran, for everything you've done for us.

Life is a journey filled with ups and downs, and navigating everyday struggles is an inherent part of this experience. Whether it's managing work stress, dealing with personal issues, or overcoming unexpected challenges, the way we handle these daily struggles shapes our resilience and overall well-being.

## Understanding Everyday Struggles

Everyday struggles come in many forms, ranging from minor inconveniences to significant life events. Common challenges include:

- Work-related stress: Deadlines, workload, and interpersonal conflicts can contribute to significant stress at work.
- Personal issues: Family dynamics, relationship problems, and health concerns can create emotional and mental strain.
- Unexpected challenges: Sudden changes, such as financial difficulties or emergencies, can disrupt daily life and require immediate attention.

Recognizing the nature and source of these struggles is the first step toward managing them effectively.

## Practical Strategies for Managing Everyday Struggles
*Prioritize Self-Care*

Self-care is essential for maintaining physical, emotional, and mental health. Incorporate the following practices into your daily routine:

- Exercise regularly: Physical activity helps reduce stress and improve mood.
- Eat a balanced diet: Proper nutrition fuels your body and mind.
- Get adequate sleep: Quality sleep is crucial for overall well-being.
- Practice mindfulness: Techniques like meditation and deep breathing can help you stay grounded.

*Organize and Plan*

Effective time management and organization can reduce the feeling of being overwhelmed. Try these tips:

- Create a daily schedule: Plan your day to ensure you allocate time for work, rest, and leisure.
- Set priorities: Focus on completing high-priority tasks first.
- Break tasks into smaller steps: This makes large projects more manageable and less daunting.
- Use tools and apps: Utilize calendars, planners, and productivity apps to stay on track.

*Develop Coping Mechanisms*

Building healthy coping mechanisms can help you handle stress more effectively:

- Practice gratitude: Reflecting on positive aspects of your life can shift your focus from problems to solutions.
- Seek social support: Connect with friends, family, or support groups to share your struggles and gain perspective.
- Engage in hobbies: Participating in activities you enjoy can provide a necessary mental break and boost your mood.

*Maintain a Positive Mindset*

Cultivating a positive mindset can enhance your resilience and help you navigate challenges with a more constructive approach.

There are times when managing struggles on your own may not be enough.

Managing everyday struggles is an ongoing process that requires patience, effort, and a proactive approach. By prioritizing self-care, organizing your time, developing healthy coping mechanisms, maintaining a positive mindset, and seeking professional help when needed, you can navigate life's challenges more effectively. Remember, it's not about avoiding struggles but learning how to handle them in a way that promotes growth and well-being. With the right strategies, you can turn everyday challenges into opportunities for personal development and resilience.

1. Stay positive. Never give up, keep moving forward, and remember, it can't rain all the time.
2. Stop trying to keep up with your neighbors. You're on a completely different path than they are.
3. Practice positive self-talk. Replace negative thoughts with encouraging and optimistic statements.
4. Set realistic goals. Achievable goals provide a sense of accomplishment and motivate you to keep moving forward.
5. Learn from setbacks: View challenges as opportunities for growth rather than obstacles.
6. Say "God, I want a refund" from how I think about daily struggles.

"Every struggle in your life has shaped you into the person you are today. Be thankful for the hard times; they can only make you stronger."
—*Keanu Reeves*

# CHAPTER 8
# LEADERSHIP SKILLS

**Putting Yourself in Your Employees' Shoes**

Imagine a young you, fresh out of school and eager to make a mark, working under the leadership of someone like yourself today. Reflecting on this scenario, it's easy to see how daunting the prospect might be. The high standards, the demand for excellence, and the drive to achieve can seem overwhelming to a young, inexperienced individual. In this light, it's not hard to envision a scenario where the young you might have found the environment so challenging that you might even contemplate firing your younger self.

This exercise in empathy underscores a fundamental aspect of effective leadership: understanding the perspective of your employees. It's crucial to remember where you started and the challenges you faced. This perspective can guide you in fostering a supportive and nurturing environment for your team.

**Developing Leadership Skills**

Empathy is the cornerstone of effective leadership. Understanding the feelings, thoughts, and perspectives of your team members helps in building trust. By putting yourself in their shoes, you can address their concerns and aspirations more effectively.

Regularly engage in one-on-one conversations with your team members. Ask about their goals, challenges, and feedback. This not only shows that you care but also provides valuable insights into improving team dynamics.

Clear and open communication is vital. It ensures that everyone is on the same page and helps in resolving conflicts swiftly. Effective communication involves not just speaking but also listening actively.

Hold regular team meetings where everyone has a chance to voice their opinions and updates. Use clear, concise language and be transparent about decisions and changes within the organization.

In the fast-paced world, change is constant. A good leader must be adaptable and open to new ideas and methods. This flexibility can inspire the same attitude in your team, making the organization more resilient and innovative.

Encourage a culture of continuous learning. Provide opportunities for professional development and be open to adopting new technologies and processes.

Holding yourself and your team accountable ensures high standards are maintained. This builds a culture of responsibility and trust. When leaders own their mistakes and successes, it sets a powerful example for the team.

Implement a system for tracking progress and performance. Regularly review goals and outcomes and address any issues constructively.

A great leader inspires a team to achieve their best. This involves setting a clear vision and motivating your team to work toward it. Inspiration comes from leading by example and showing passion and commitment to your work.

Share success stories and celebrate achievements. Show your team the impact of their work and how it contributes to the larger goals of the organization.

Making timely and well-informed decisions is another key leadership skill. Decisiveness helps in moving projects forward and addressing issues promptly. It also instills confidence in your team.

When faced with decisions, gather all necessary information, consult with relevant team members, and then make a choice. Communicate your decision clearly and explain the rationale behind it.

**Leading the Young You**

Leading a young version of yourself would undoubtedly come with challenges. The high energy, ambition, and occasional overconfidence of youth need to be harnessed and guided effectively. Here are some specific strategies:

- Mentorship: Offer guidance and share your experiences. Mentorship helps young employees navigate their career paths and avoid common pitfalls.
- Structured Feedback: Provide regular constructive feedback. Young employees need to know what they are doing right and where they need improvement.
- Opportunities for Growth: Create opportunities for young employees to take on new responsibilities and learn new skills. This keeps them engaged and fosters professional development.
- Encouragement and Support: Recognize their achievements and offer support when they face challenges. A little encouragement can go a long way in boosting morale and confidence.

Reflecting on how you would have fared under your own leadership can be a humbling experience. It highlights the importance of empathy, communication, adaptability, accountability, inspiration, and decisiveness in effective leadership. By continuously developing these skills, you can create a supportive and productive environment for your team, helping each member reach their full potential.

If someone comes into your office and starts telling you something that one of their coworkers has done, tell them, "Hang on one second. I'll be right back." Go get the person they are talking about, bring them into your office, and say, "OK, we were just about to talk about you." Look at the employee who is making the complaint and say, "Continue." I've done this before, and it worked great. Everyone gets to voice their opinions without all of the "he said, she said" drama that usually occurs in workplaces. It encourages transparency and allows for immediate resolution of conflicts.

Trust the people you work with and give them the space to grow and learn from their experiences. Remember how you once felt when you made a mistake and were worried about your employment. I'm betting you were a nervous wreck and couldn't sleep or eat anything for days. In leadership positions, we have to put ourselves in our employees' shoes.

1. Put yourself in your employees' shoes.
2. Imagine talking to a younger you. How would you feel?
3. Try getting both sides of the story at the same time.
4. A little encouragement can go a long way.
5. Never ask someone to do something you wouldn't do.
6. Say "God, I want a refund" from people who let leadership positions go to their head.

"Before you abuse, criticize, and accuse / Walk a mile in my shoes."
—*Elvis Presley*

# CHAPTER 9
# THE POWER OF HELPING OTHERS

In a world that often feels divided and isolated, the act of helping others stands as a beacon of hope and connection. Whether through small acts of kindness or grand gestures of support, helping others can transform lives, foster communities, and create a ripple effect of positivity. This chapter delves into the importance of helping others, exploring its benefits, the different ways we can lend a hand, and how this selfless practice can lead to a more fulfilling life.

## The Benefits of Helping Others
- Emotional Well-being: Helping others has been shown to enhance our own emotional well-being. When we assist someone in need, our brain releases endorphins, creating a "helper's high." This feeling of satisfaction and happiness can reduce stress, alleviate anxiety, and combat feelings of depression.
- Building Connections: Acts of kindness strengthen our social bonds. Whether it's helping a neighbor with broken pipes or helping someone out with their groceries, these interactions foster a sense of community and belonging. Strong social connections are linked to increased longevity and improved overall health.
- Personal Growth: Helping others provides opportunities for personal growth and self-discovery. It allows us to step out of our comfort zones, develop empathy, and gain new perspec-

tives. Through these experiences, we can better understand our strengths and weaknesses and grow as individuals.

- Creating Positive Change: When we help others, we contribute to creating a positive change in society. Acts of kindness can inspire others to do the same, leading to a culture of generosity and compassion. This collective effort can address social issues, support vulnerable populations, and build a more inclusive and supportive community.

My wife's lifelong friend, Julie, was determined to become a nurse. One night over dinner, she shared her excitement about her phlebotomy class and how crucial it was for her to practice drawing blood on real people. Natalie, always eager to support her friend, suggested that I might volunteer to be her practice subject.

I wasn't thrilled about the idea at first. The thought of a needle going into my arm from someone who has never stuck anyone before made me a bit uneasy, but seeing Julie's passion and determination won me over. One Saturday afternoon, we set up a makeshift clinic in our living room. Julie grabbed her kit, wearing a nervous but determined smile.

As Julie prepared her equipment, Natalie sat beside me, holding my hand for support. Julie explained each step of the process, her voice steady despite her visible nerves. She swabbed my arm with alcohol while Natalie squeezed my hand reassuringly.

Julie's first attempt wasn't perfect. She missed the vein, and I winced as she adjusted. But instead of giving up, she took a deep breath, reassured herself, and tried again. This time, she found the vein, and the blood flowed into the vial smoothly.

Natalie beamed with pride, and Julie's face lit up with relief and joy. It wasn't just a simple blood draw; it was a small victory that represented her hard work and determination. Over the next few weeks, Julie practiced on me several more times, and each time she grew more confident and skilled.

Those sessions became more than just practice for Julie; they turned into moments of bonding and support among the three of us. It was a privilege to be a part of Julie's journey, watching her transform from a nervous student into a confident and capable nurse. And through it all, Natalie's unwavering support and my small act of bravery helped a friend achieve her dreams. Julie passed away suddenly right after I began writing this. Her passion for helping others has truly inspired me to write this chapter and finish this book.

## Ways to Help Others

- Acts of Kindness: Small, everyday acts of kindness can have a significant impact. Holding the door open for someone, offering a listening ear, or even a simple smile can brighten someone's day and make them feel valued and appreciated.
- Financial Support: Donating money to individuals in need is another powerful way to help. Financial contributions can fund important projects, provide essential resources, and offer relief to those facing hardships.
- Mentorship and Education: Sharing our knowledge and expertise can help others achieve their goals and overcome challenges. Mentoring a young person, offering career advice, or teaching a new skill are all ways to make a lasting impact.
- Advocacy: Sometimes, helping others means advocating for their rights and needs. This can involve raising awareness about social issues or supporting policies that promote equity and justice.

## Overcoming Barriers to Helping Others

Despite our best intentions, there can be barriers that prevent us from helping others. Recognizing and addressing these obstacles is crucial to fostering a culture of selflessness.

- Time Constraints: Busy schedules can make it challenging to find time for others. However, even small gestures can make a difference. Setting aside a few minutes each day for acts of kindness can integrate helping others into our routines.
- Fear of Rejection: The fear of our help being rejected or unappreciated can deter us from reaching out. It's important to remember that the act of offering help itself is valuable, regardless of the outcome. Reaching out with genuine intent can often be more impactful than we realize.
- Lack of Resources: We may feel that we lack the resources to make a significant difference. However, help comes in many

forms, and often, our time, attention, and skills are more valuable than material resources.

## Stories of Helping Others
### The Story of Don

Don, a retiree from the military, started volunteering at a local school, helping children with their skills. Over the years, he has seen countless students improve their literacy and confidence. One student in particular struggled with reading but, through Don's consistent support, became an avid reader and went on to excel academically.

### A Small Community

In the growing town of Southaven, a city worker helped out an elderly community. They had fencing that was down and a slew of problems that were not the city's responsibility. So he went after work on his own time and helped put the fencing back up, fixed the landscaping, and much more. He never told anyone.

### A Simple Gesture

Jeremy, a busy government employee, noticed his coworker struggling with his yard work. He offered to help, and from that small act, a friendship blossomed. Jeremy learned about his coworker's life, his health challenges, and his joys. Their bond grew, and it became a source of mutual support and encouragement. Jeremy is now the godfather to my youngest son.

Looking back as a teenager, I remember growing up with almost nothing, wearing the same clothes every day. Then, church members came together and bought me several new outfits. I was so proud of those clothes that I wore them every day. To those kindhearted people, I am forever grateful. You know who you are, and I will never forget your acts of kindness.

I was always self-conscious about my teeth. They were crooked and misaligned, and I knew they stood out. One day, a guy sneered at me and said, "Your teeth look like they're throwing gang signs." Years later, I met Natalie and her parents. They were kind and welcoming, but I couldn't shake my embarrassment about my teeth. After Natalie and I got married, during a family dinner, Natalie's mother noticed my reluctance to smile and gently asked about it. Hesitantly, I shared my lifelong insecurity.

A few weeks later, Natalie's parents sat me down.

Her mother spoke first. "We've been thinking about what you said, and we want to help." They explained that they wanted to pay for me to get my teeth fixed. I was overwhelmed by their generosity.

The day the braces came off, I couldn't stop smiling. My teeth were straight, and for the first time in years, I felt confident. I thanked my in-laws profusely, grateful not just for the gift of a new smile but for their kindness and love. I no longer had to hide my smile; it was replaced by the warmth of family and the confidence to smile freely.

Helping others is a powerful force that can transform our lives and the world around us. By offering our time, resources, and kindness, we can create a ripple effect of positivity that extends far beyond our immediate actions. Whether through grand gestures or small acts, the impact of helping others is profound and enduring. As we navigate our lives, let us remember the words of Mahatma Gandhi: "The best way to find yourself is to lose yourself in the service of others." By embracing this philosophy, we can build a more compassionate, connected, and resilient world.

1. Recognize the need for help.
2. Understand the situation before offering help. It's important to understand the context and specific needs of the person.
3. Follow through. If you commit to help someone, follow through with your promise.
4. If you're unable to help directly, consider other ways to support, such as connecting the person with someone who can.
5. Help someone out and don't post online or brag about it. Stop running around telling everyone what you've done. Don't do it to be glorified.
6. Say "God, I want a refund" from every time I've hesitate to help others, from every time I've struggled with selfish thoughts.

"Never worry about numbers. Help one person at a time and always start with the person nearest you."
—*Mother Teresa*

# CHAPTER 10
# THE POWER OF FORGIVENESS

Forgiveness is a profound and transformative concept that has been explored by philosophers, theologians, and psychologists for centuries. At its core, forgiveness is the act of letting go of resentment, anger, and the desire for retribution against those who have wronged us. It is a conscious decision to release negative emotions and replace them with understanding, compassion, and empathy.

### The Nature of Forgiveness

Forgiveness is often misunderstood. It is not about condoning or excusing harmful behavior, nor is it about forgetting the wrongs done to us. Instead, forgiveness is a personal process that involves recognizing the pain caused by someone else's actions and choosing to move past it. It is about freeing ourselves from the emotional burden of carrying grudges and enabling ourselves to heal and grow.

### The Psychological Benefits of Forgiveness

Studies have shown that forgiveness has significant psychological benefits. Holding on to anger and resentment can lead to chronic stress, anxiety, and depression. By contrast, forgiveness can reduce stress, lower blood pressure, and improve overall mental health. It allows us to break free from the cycle of negativity and promotes emotional well-being.

## The Process of Forgiveness

Forgiveness is not a one-time event but a journey. Here are the key steps involved in this process:

- Acknowledging the Hurt: Recognizing and accepting the pain caused by someone else's actions is the first step. This involves understanding the impact of the offense on our lives and emotions.
- Empathy and Understanding: Trying to see the situation from the offender's perspective can foster empathy. This doesn't mean excusing their behavior but understanding the possible reasons behind it.
- Deciding to Forgive: Forgiveness is a conscious choice. It involves deciding to let go of the anger and resentment, even if the offender has not apologized or shown remorse.
- Releasing Negative Emotions: This step involves expressing and releasing the negative emotions associated with the hurt. This can be done through talking, writing, or other forms of self-expression.
- Finding Peace and Moving Forward: The final step is to find peace within ourselves and move forward. This doesn't necessarily mean reconciling with the offender but finding a way to live without the burden of past grievances.

## Forgiveness in Relationships

Forgiveness plays a crucial role in maintaining healthy relationships. In any relationship, misunderstandings and conflicts are inevitable. Forgiveness helps repair the damage caused by these conflicts and strengthens the bond between individuals. It fosters trust, empathy, and mutual respect, allowing relationships to flourish.

## Self-Forgiveness

Just as important as forgiving others is the ability to forgive ourselves. We are often our harshest critics, and self-forgiveness is essential for personal growth and self-compassion. Acknowledging our mistakes, learning from them, and choosing to let go of self-blame enables us to move forward with a healthier mindset.

### The Spiritual Dimension of Forgiveness

Many spiritual traditions emphasize the importance of forgiveness. In Christianity, for instance, forgiveness is a central tenet, with teachings that emphasize the need to forgive others as God forgives us.

### Challenges to Forgiveness

Forgiveness can be challenging, especially when the hurt is deep or the offender is unrepentant. Common obstacles include:

- Pride and Ego: Sometimes our pride and ego make it difficult to forgive. We may see forgiveness as a sign of weakness or fear that it diminishes our sense of justice.
- Fear of Vulnerability: Forgiving someone can make us feel vulnerable, as it involves letting go of our defenses and opening ourselves up to potential future hurt.
- Misunderstanding Forgiveness: Many people believe that forgiving means condoning the offense or reconciling with the offender. This misconception can prevent them from embracing forgiveness.

### The Ripple Effect of Forgiveness

Forgiveness has a ripple effect that extends beyond the individual. When we forgive, we contribute to a more compassionate and understanding world. Our actions can inspire others to forgive and create a culture of empathy and kindness. In this way, forgiveness has the power to transform not just our lives but the lives of those around us.

### Forgiveness Can Be Hard Sometimes

As my Mamaw laid in her bed, battling cancer, I spent hours by her side, holding her hand, and whispering words of comfort, though I knew she was the one comforting me.

My father was a ghost in our lives, appearing sporadically. The drugs had taken hold of him, reducing the man I once knew to a shadow of himself. Despite everything, I still held on to the hope that he would come around, that the father we believed he could be would emerge from the fog of addiction.

One evening as I returned from visiting my Mamaw at the hospital, I got a call from my cousin Josh. He said, "Robert, your dad's taken your mamaw's car."

I said to him, "He's going to pawn it for drugs. We need to find him."

Rage and despair coursed through me. How could he do this—now, of all times? Mamaw needed us, needed our strength and support. And my father, lost in his addiction, was about to betray her in the worst possible way.

Josh and I drove through the night, searching the parts of town where we knew my father might be. The streets were filled with people who had lost their way, and it pained me to think my father was one of them. After what felt like an eternity, we spotted Mamaw's car. My heart pounded in my chest as I saw my father.

Without thinking, I jumped out of our car and ran toward him. "Dad, stop!" I shouted. He turned to face me, his eyes wild and unfocused. For a moment, I saw a flicker of recognition, but it was quickly replaced by the desperate look of a man who would do anything for his next fix.

Before I could reach him, he jumped in the car and started the engine. I stood in front of the car, arms outstretched, pleading with him to stop. "Please, Dad. Don't do this."

But then his desperation took over. He hit the gas, and the car lurched forward, hitting me and knocking me to the ground. Pain shot through my body, but it was nothing compared to the agony in my heart as I watched him drive away.

Josh helped me up, and we stood there in stunned silence, the reality of what had just happened sinking in. My own father had run me down, choosing his addiction over his family. It was a betrayal that cut deeper than any physical wound.

For a long time after that night, I struggled with my anger and resentment. I couldn't understand how he could do such a thing to his own son, how he could hurt us so deeply. But as time passed, I began to see the truth: it wasn't really him. It was the drugs. The addiction had turned him into someone I didn't recognize, someone who wasn't capable of thinking clearly or making rational decisions.

Eventually, my father did the right thing. He returned the car, and though it was a small gesture, it was a step toward redemption. Slowly, painfully, I learned to forgive him. I had to—for my own sake as much as for his.

Forgiveness didn't come easily, but it brought with it a sense of peace. I couldn't change the past. I couldn't undo the hurt and the betrayal. But I could choose to let go of the anger and find a way to move forward. In forgiving him, I found a way to heal, to reclaim a part of myself that had been lost in the darkness of his addiction.

I could tell you a hundred different stories like that, but now is not the time for those stories. Not yet.

Forgiveness is a powerful tool for personal and relational healing. It is a journey that requires courage, empathy, and a willingness to let go of past hurts. By embracing forgiveness, we can free ourselves from the chains of resentment, foster healthier relationships, and contribute to a more compassionate world.

1. Recognize and accept the pain caused by someone else's actions. Only then can you truly forgive them.
2. Let go of the anger and resentment, even if the offender has not apologized or shown remorse.
3. Swallow your pride and put your ego away. Understand that forgiveness is for your own peace and well-being, not necessarily for reconciliation.
4. Open your heart and try to see the situation from the other person's perspective.
5. Remember there are always three sides to every story: yours, theirs, and the truth.
6. Say "God, I want a refund" from every grudge I've held, regretting all the time lost in anger.

"When a deep injury is done to us, we never heal until we forgive."
—*Nelson Mandela*

# CHAPTER 11
# EMBRACING CHANGE AND REJECTING NEGATIVITY

**Introduction**

Life is an unpredictable journey filled with both joyous moments and challenging times. While we cannot control everything that happens to us, we do have power over how we respond and the choices we make. Embracing change and refusing to accept negativity as a permanent part of our lives can lead to profound personal growth and a more fulfilling existence.

We have to change how we treat each other. I'll be the first to admit that I used to bust others down when they were being hypocritical and call them out on their faults. Well, that's bullying, and I can't stand a bully. In situations like this, I've learned that it's best to keep your two cents in your pocket.

Bullying is a pervasive issue that affects children in schools across the globe. It is a behavior that can have lasting effects on both the victim and the perpetrator. As a society, we often emphasize the importance of teaching children to be kind, empathetic, and respectful. However, there is a significant disconnect when adults engage in behaviors that contradict these teachings. This chapter explores the critical role of adult behavior in shaping the social dynamics of younger generations and the urgent need to model positive interactions.

### The Mirror Effect: Children Reflecting Adult Behavior

Children are remarkably perceptive and often mirror the behaviors they observe in adults. This phenomenon, known as the mirror effect, highlights the importance of role models in a child's development. When adults exhibit bullying behaviors—whether it be verbal abuse, social exclusion, or physical intimidation—children take note. They learn that such actions are acceptable and may mimic them in their interactions with peers.

### The Hypocrisy of "Do as I Say, Not as I Do"

One of the most glaring issues in addressing bullying is the hypocritical stance many adults take. We tell children to be kind, to refrain from name-calling, and to include everyone, yet our own actions often tell a different story. Adults may engage in workplace bullying, participate in online harassment, or even demonstrate aggression in personal relationships. This inconsistency sends a confusing message to children: bullying is only wrong when they do it, not when adults do it.

### The Power of Mindset

*Understanding Mindset*

Your mindset shapes your reality. A fixed mindset limits your potential by making you believe that your abilities and circumstances are static. In contrast, a growth mindset encourages you to see challenges as opportunities for learning and development.

*Cultivating a Growth Mindset*

Embrace the belief that you can change and improve. Celebrate small victories, learn from failures, and stay open to new experiences. This shift in perspective can transform how you approach life's challenges.

### Identifying and Eliminating Negativity

*Recognizing Negative Influences*

Identify sources of negativity in your life, whether they are toxic relationships, unfulfilling jobs, or harmful habits. Acknowledge how these factors affect your well-being and take steps to minimize their impact.

*Setting Boundaries*

Establish clear boundaries to protect your mental and emotional health. Learn to say no to situations and people that drain your energy. Surround yourself with positive influences that uplift and inspire you.

## Embracing Change

*Embracing Uncertainty*

Change often involves stepping into the unknown, which can be daunting. Embrace uncertainty as a natural part of growth. Remember, every significant change starts with a decision to try something new.

*Setting Goals and Taking Action*

Define what you want to change in your life and set specific, achievable goals. Break these goals into manageable steps and take consistent action. Progress, no matter how small, builds momentum and confidence.

After years of struggling with the weight of past traumas and heartache, my mother finally decided it was time to reclaim her life. Her journey had been a long one, marked by moments of despair and flickers of hope. She had always been a fighter, but the battles had worn her down, leaving her a shadow of the vibrant woman she once was.

The toll it had taken on her was evident. The light in her eyes had dimmed, and her laughter became a rare sound in our home. I watched her suffer, feeling powerless to help, until one day, something within her shifted. It was as if she had reached the end of her tether and realized that she deserved more than the life she was living.

She started taking care of herself again, finding solace in activities she once loved. Slowly but surely, she began to rediscover her strength and resilience.

And then one day, she met Gill. Gill was different from anyone she had ever known. He was kind, patient, and understanding. He saw my mother not as who she was but as who she could be. He admired her courage and the way she had fought for herself. Gill was the kind of man who listened more than he spoke and offered a steady presence that made my mother feel safe.

Their relationship blossomed gradually. Gill never rushed her, allowing her to set the pace. He understood the scars she carried and helped her heal with his gentle, unwavering support. With Gill by her side, my mother began to believe in love again.

It wasn't just about finding a new partner; it was about my mother reclaiming her life.

## Building Resilience
### Developing Resilience
Resilience is the ability to bounce back from adversity. Cultivate resilience by maintaining a positive outlook, practicing self-care, and seeking support from others. Resilient individuals view setbacks as temporary and solvable.

### Learning from Adversity
Reflect on past challenges and consider what they taught you. Use these lessons to inform your future decisions. Adversity can be a powerful teacher, providing insights and strengthening your character.

## Practicing Gratitude and Positivity
### Gratitude Journaling
Keep a gratitude journal to regularly acknowledge and appreciate the positive aspects of your life. Writing down what you are thankful for can shift your focus from what's wrong to what's right.

### Positive Affirmations
Incorporate positive affirmations into your daily routine. Affirmations are powerful statements that reinforce your goals and values. By repeating them, you can rewire your brain to adopt a more optimistic outlook.

## Embracing Self-Compassion
### Be Kind to Yourself
Practice self-compassion by treating yourself with the same kindness and understanding you would offer a friend. Accept that mistakes and setbacks are part of the human experience.

*Self-Care Rituals*

Establish self-care rituals that nurture your body, mind, and soul. This could include activities like meditation, exercise, reading, or spending time in nature. Prioritizing self-care is essential for maintaining balance and well-being.

## Creating a Supportive Environment

*Building a Support Network*

Surround yourself with people who encourage and support your growth. Share your goals and progress with trusted friends or mentors. A strong support network can provide motivation, accountability, and guidance.

*Seeking Professional Help*

If you find it difficult to navigate change or overcome negativity on your own, consider seeking professional help. Therapists, coaches, and counselors can offer valuable insights and strategies tailored to your needs.

Changing your life and rejecting negativity requires commitment, courage, and patience. It's a journey of continuous self-improvement and discovery. By adopting a growth mindset, setting clear goals, and surrounding yourself with positive influences, you can create a life that aligns with your true potential. Remember, the power to change lies within you, and every step you take brings you closer to a brighter, more fulfilling future.

> "Believe you can and you're halfway there."
> —*attributed to Theodore Roosevelt*

1. Be humble, stay hungry, and be the hardest worker in the room.
2. Stop looking for validation from others. The only person you need permission from to do something is you.
3. Stop trying to keep up with others and live your own life. Embrace failure as a learning experience. Every setback is a chance to grow stronger and wiser.
4. Practice self-compassion and stop being so hard on yourself. Tell yourself every day, "I'm stronger than this situation."

5. Remember, the power to change lies within you. Believe in yourself and be who you are meant to be.

6. "God, I want a refund" from every time I said something that hurt someone else. I wish I could take back every careless word, every misunderstanding. It's never too late to say, "I'm Sorry."

"The secret of change is to focus all of your energy not on fighting the old, but on building the new."
—*Dan Millman*

# CHAPTER 12
# STOP PUTTING THINGS OFF

In a world where opportunities are abundant and distractions are omnipresent, achieving our goals can often seem like a daunting task. Yet the essence of success lies in one simple principle: don't procrastinate with your goals. Get up and go after them.

Every journey has its challenges, and mine was no different. When I think about building guitars and recording songs, there's one truth that stands out above all else: I never would have built any guitars or recorded a single song if I had given in to "I just don't feel like it today."

I remember the first time I held a piece of wood that would become a guitar. It was raw, unshaped, and full of potential—much like my dreams. But dreams don't come to life through wishes alone; they require relentless effort, even on days when motivation is scarce.

Doubt is a persistent adversary. It whispers in your ear, questioning your abilities and the worth of your endeavors. In those early days, I faced countless moments where doubt crept in. My first attempts at crafting a guitar were far from perfect. There were times when the wood split, the strings snapped, and my hands hurt from hours of sanding and shaping. Each setback was a test of my resolve.

Does your wife ever ask you to do something for her, like help her out by taking out the trash, and you say, "Yeah, I'll get to it shortly"? Then it gets full, and she just takes it out herself. You find yourself on the defensive side, and you say, "I was going to do that." She says, "Don't worry about it. I got it." We've all had that fight. Stop procrastinating.

## The Cost of Procrastination

Procrastination isn't just a harmless habit; it's a significant barrier to personal and professional growth. When you procrastinate, you:

- Miss Opportunities: Many opportunities have a shelf life. Waiting too long to act can mean missing out on potentially life-changing chances.
- Increase Stress: Unfinished tasks weigh heavily on your mind, increasing stress and anxiety.
- Lower Your Self-Esteem: Consistent procrastination can lead to feelings of inadequacy and self-doubt.
- Hinder Personal Growth: Delaying action stalls your progress and keeps you from realizing your potential.

Understanding the cost of procrastination is the first step in motivating yourself to overcome it. Recognize that each moment of delay is a moment lost in achieving your goals.

## The Mindset Shift: From Procrastination to Action

To conquer procrastination, you must shift your mindset. Here's how to develop an action-oriented mindset:

- Set Clear, Achievable Goals: Break down your larger goals into smaller, manageable tasks. This makes them less intimidating and more attainable.
- Embrace Imperfection: Understand that perfection is a myth. Strive for progress, not perfection. Taking action, even if it's imperfect, is better than inaction.
- Cultivate Self-Discipline: Discipline is the bridge between goals and accomplishment. Build habits that foster discipline, such as setting specific times for working on your goals and sticking to them.
- Visualize Success: Imagine the satisfaction and rewards of achieving your goals. Visualization can be a powerful motivator.

**Practical Strategies to Stop Procrastination**

Implement these strategies to move from procrastination to productivity:

- The Two-Minute Rule: If a task will take less than two minutes to complete, do it immediately. This helps build momentum and reduces the pile-up of small tasks.
- Time Blocking: Allocate specific blocks of time to work on different tasks. This ensures focused effort and reduces the temptation to procrastinate.
- Eliminate Distractions: Identify what commonly distracts you and take steps to minimize these distractions. This could mean turning off notifications, setting a specific workspace, or using productivity apps.
- Accountability Partners: Share your goals with a trusted friend or colleague. They can provide encouragement and hold you accountable for your progress.
- Reward Yourself: Set up a reward system for completing tasks. This provides an additional incentive to get things done.

Seriously—put the phone down and go get started.

Consider the stories of successful individuals who achieved greatness by overcoming procrastination:

*Steve Jobs*

Known for his relentless pursuit of innovation, Jobs didn't wait for the perfect moment or product. He took action, iterated, and improved, leading Apple to become a technology giant.

*J. K. Rowling*

Despite numerous rejections, Rowling continued to write and submit her work. Her perseverance paid off, making *Harry Potter* a global phenomenon.

*Elon Musk*

Musk's ventures into electric cars, space travel, and renewable energy have been filled with risks and challenges. His commitment to action, despite uncertainties, has revolutionized multiple industries.

Don't procrastinate. When you get home, take care of everything you want to do for the evening right away. Don't walk through the door and plop down on the couch or in your favorite recliner. If you do, you'll look up and realize you've spent hours on your phone, surrounding yourself with negativity from the news or social media. You'll wonder, where did all the time go? You'll never have time for yourself if you constantly give it away to social media or television.

- Build Momentum: Taking the first step creates momentum. Each subsequent step becomes easier as you build on your initial action.
- Break the Fear Barrier: Procrastination often stems from fear—fear of failure, fear of the unknown, or fear of imperfection. By just doing it, you confront and overcome these fears.
- Create Learning Opportunities: Action, whether successful or not, provides valuable learning experiences. You gain insights and skills that prepare you for future challenges.
- Foster a Growth Mindset: Embracing action over inaction cultivates a growth mindset where you see challenges as opportunities to grow rather than obstacles to avoid.

**Your Journey Begins Now**

Procrastination is a formidable adversary, but it's one you can defeat. By understanding its costs, shifting your mindset, and implementing practical strategies, you can transform your approach to achieving your goals. Remember, the key is to just do it. Take that first step today—no matter how small—and set yourself on the path to success. Your future self will thank you.

In the end, the journey of a thousand miles begins with a single step. Don't let procrastination hold you back. Embrace action, and watch your dreams turn into reality.

Step 1: Don't procrastinate on your goals. Get up and go after them.

Step 2: Many opportunities have a shelf life. Go after them right now.

Step 3: Overcome your fears and don't be afraid of failing.

Step 4: Believe in your ability to make progress, no matter how slow.

Step 5: Maintain consistency and track your progress regularly.

Step 6: "God, I want a refund" from every time I put something off and it kept me from reaching my potential.

"Do not put off until tomorrow what can be done today."
—*attributed to the Greek poet Hesiod*

# CHAPTER 13
# DON'T LET YOUR PAST KEEP YOU FROM YOUR FUTURE

Everyone has a past filled with memories, experiences, and decisions—some joyous, others painful. Our past shapes who we are, but it doesn't have to dictate our future. Often, we find ourselves shackled by past mistakes, regrets, or traumas, unable to move forward.

### Rising Above the Shadows

If I had let all the circumstances from my childhood hold me back, I'd be in a very different place right now. Childhood has a profound impact on shaping our personalities and paths in life, and for many, the journey through those early years is fraught with challenges that can leave lasting scars.

Growing up, I faced numerous obstacles. Maybe it was the financial instability that kept our family on edge, never knowing if we'd make it through the month. Perhaps it was the emotional turmoil from a household torn apart by my parents' drug use, or it could have been the constant feeling of being an outsider, always struggling to fit in and find my place.

Had I given in to these situations, my present would be much darker and filled with unfulfilled potential. I would likely be trapped in a cycle of self-doubt and fear, unable to break free from the chains of the past. Every step forward would be hindered by the weight of unresolved traumas, and the dreams I once held would remain distant and unattainable.

Without the resolve to rise above, I might have settled for a life of mediocrity, accepting less than what I deserved because it seemed easier than fighting for more. My potential would have been stifled, and the achievements that define my current existence would be mere fantasies.

But I didn't let those circumstances define me. Instead, I chose to rise above. I used those circumstances as fuel to propel me forward. I learned that adversity can be a powerful teacher, shaping resilience and determination. Each setback became a stepping stone, each hardship a lesson in perseverance. By facing my past head-on and refusing to be its victim, I forged a path toward a brighter future.

Today, I stand as a testament to the strength of the human spirit. I have achieved more than I once thought possible, not in spite of my past but because of it. The challenges I faced didn't hold me back; they pushed me to grow, to strive for excellence, and to never settle for anything less than my best.

If I had let my childhood circumstances dictate my life, I wouldn't be the person I am today. I wouldn't have the same depth of understanding, empathy, and resilience. I wouldn't have the drive to succeed or the appreciation for the journey. My past could have been my prison, but instead, it became the foundation upon which I built my future.

Growing up in a chaotic environment created by my parents' addictions was a struggle that tested me in ways I could never have imagined. My childhood was marked by instability, uncertainty, and a sense of abandonment. Yet amid this turmoil, I found a determination to break the cycle and create a better life for myself and my future family.

I remember vividly the nights when my father would disappear, leaving my mother and me in a state of fear and confusion. His addiction to drugs controlled his life, and it often felt like it controlled ours too. With my mother also battling her own demons, I learned early on that if I wanted a different life, I would have to forge it myself.

Knowing that my lack of education was going to hold me back, I worked hard and completed my GED, often juggling part-time jobs to support myself and save for a future that I hoped would be different. It wasn't easy; there were times when I felt defeated.

As I grew older, I met someone who would change my life forever. She was kind, understanding, and supportive. Together, we dreamed of building a family based on love, trust, and stability. When we got married, I vowed that our children would never experience the hardships I had endured.

When our children were both born, I was filled with a mixture of joy and fear. Joy because I had finally achieved something I had always longed for—a family of my own. Fear because I knew the responsibility that came with it. But every time I look at my children, I am reminded of why I fought so hard. I was determined to provide them with the security and love that had been absent in my own upbringing.

Parenthood was a learning curve, but I embraced it wholeheartedly. I made sure to be present, to listen, and to support my children in every way possible. I wanted them to know that they were valued and loved, no matter what. I also wanted to teach them about resilience and the importance of perseverance.

Throughout this journey, I maintained a sense of forgiveness toward my parents. Their addiction was a disease that they couldn't control, and while it caused me immense pain, it also shaped me into the person I am today. I chose to learn from their mistakes rather than be defined by them.

Looking back, I realize that my parents' addictions, while devastating, also fueled my determination to create a different path. I broke free from the cycle, and in doing so, I built a life filled with love, stability, and hope. My children will never know the struggles I faced, but they will know the strength and resilience that it took to overcome them.

In the end, it's not about where we come from but where we choose to go. I chose to build a family grounded in love and support. And in that choice, I found redemption, healing, and the fulfillment of a dream that once seemed impossible.

## Understanding the Impact of the Past

The past holds a powerful influence over us. It's the foundation of our beliefs, attitudes, and behaviors. Positive experiences can boost our confidence and resilience, while negative ones can leave us feeling stuck, ashamed, or fearful. Understanding how your past affects you is the first step toward liberation.

*Acknowledge Your Past*

Denying or repressing past experiences doesn't make them disappear. Instead, it often leads to unresolved issues resurfacing in harmful ways. Acknowledge what has happened, whether it's a mistake, a failure, or a trauma. Acceptance is crucial for healing.

*Identify Limiting Beliefs*

Limiting beliefs are negative thoughts and assumptions formed from past experiences that hinder your progress. These could be thoughts like "I'm not good enough," "I always fail," or "I don't deserve happiness." Identifying these beliefs is essential so that you can challenge and change them.

## The Power of Perspective

Changing how you view your past can transform your future. Your experiences are not just a series of events but lessons that have contributed to your growth and resilience.

*Reframe Your Narrative*

Instead of seeing your past as a series of failures or regrets, view it as a journey of growth. Each mistake is a lesson learned, each hardship an opportunity to develop strength and empathy. Reframing your narrative helps you see value in your experiences.

*Forgiveness and Compassion*

Forgiving yourself and others is a powerful step toward releasing the past. Holding on to grudges or self-blame keeps you anchored in negative emotions. Practice self-compassion and forgive those who have wronged you. This doesn't mean condoning harmful behavior but freeing yourself from the burden of resentment.

## Setting Your Future in Motion

Once you've acknowledged your past and shifted your perspective, it's time to set your future in motion. Your past does not define your future; your actions and choices do.

*Set Clear Goals*

Define what you want for your future. Setting clear, achievable goals gives you direction and purpose. Break down your goals into smaller, manageable steps to avoid feeling overwhelmed.

*Create a Plan*

Develop a strategic plan to achieve your goals. This plan should include actionable steps, timelines, and resources needed. Having a plan keeps you focused and motivated.

*Seek Support*

Surround yourself with a supportive network of friends, family, or mentors. Seek professional help if needed, such as therapy or counseling. Support systems provide encouragement, accountability, and different perspectives.

**Embracing Change and Growth**

Embracing your future requires a willingness to change and grow. This might mean stepping out of your comfort zone and taking risks.

*Cultivate Resilience*

Life will always have challenges, but resilience helps you bounce back stronger. Cultivate resilience by maintaining a positive outlook, staying adaptable, and learning from setbacks.

*Practice Mindfulness*

Mindfulness keeps you grounded in the present moment, reducing the tendency to dwell on the past or worry about the future. Techniques like meditation, deep breathing, and mindful activities help you stay focused and calm.

*Celebrate Progress*

Acknowledge and celebrate your achievements, no matter how small. Celebrating progress reinforces positive behavior and keeps you motivated.

We've all done things that we're not proud of. You don't have to confess your sins to anyone but God and yourself. Learn from them and move on. Find peace no matter how stressful life gets. Remember, as long as the foundation is good, then everything else will be OK. I promise.

"When you get yourself in a rut, you have to pull yourself out. You have to attach yourself to something stronger than the ruts." —John Frank Morgan

Your past is a part of you, but it doesn't have to define your future. By acknowledging your past, reframing your narrative, setting clear goals, and embracing change, you can break free from the chains of your past and create a future filled with promise and possibility. Every day is a new opportunity to start afresh, to make new choices, and to move closer to the life you envision for yourself. Don't let your past keep you from your future—embrace it, learn from it, and use it as a stepping stone to a brighter tomorrow.

1. Stop worrying about the past. Worries will only consume you.
2. Don't beat yourself up over your past. Move forward, don't look back, and let the past stay in the past.
3. Remember that each mistake is a lesson learned.
4. Don't let another person's small mistake ruin a lifetime of success.
5. Be thankful and say thank you for all the positive aspects of your life, no matter how small they may seem.
6. "God, I want a refund" from every time I let the past hold me back or cloud my judgment, from every moment I doubted my worth, from every opportunity I missed due to fear.

"If we all had a time machine we would use it. We all have regrets."
—Dave Pentecost

# CHAPTER 14
## DON'T BELIEVE EVERYTHING YOU HEAR

In today's world, the phrase "don't believe everything you see on the news" has become a crucial reminder for anyone navigating the vast and often overwhelming landscape of information. While the news is a vital source of information, it is essential to approach it with a critical mind.

### The Nature of Modern News

Modern news media outlets operate under intense pressure to capture viewers' attention. With the rise of twenty-four-hour news cycles and the competition for clicks and ratings, news outlets sometimes prioritize sensationalism over accuracy. Headlines are designed to grab attention, often at the expense of nuance and context. This environment can lead to the spread of misinformation and the distortion of facts.

### Bias and Perspective

Every news outlet has a perspective shaped by its editorial stance, ownership, and target audience. This inherent bias can influence how stories are reported and which stories are chosen for coverage. For example, one network might highlight a story about economic growth while another focuses on economic inequality. Neither is necessarily wrong, but each presents a partial view of reality.

### The Role of Social Media

Social media platforms have transformed how news is consumed and shared. Algorithms designed to maximize engagement often prioritize sensational or controversial content, which can lead to the rapid spread of misinformation. Additionally, the echo chamber effect means people are more likely to see news that aligns with their preexisting beliefs, reinforcing biases and making it harder to see the full picture.

### The Power of Visuals

Images and videos are powerful tools in storytelling, but they can also be misleading. A photograph captures a single moment in time, often without context. Videos can be edited to emphasize particular aspects or exclude important details. In the digital age, doctored AI images and deep fakes—videos altered using artificial intelligence—have become sophisticated enough to fool even the discerning eye.

### Critical Thinking and Media Literacy

To navigate the complexities of modern news, media literacy is essential. This involves understanding how news is produced, recognizing bias, and evaluating sources critically. Here are some strategies to help you become a more discerning consumer of news:

- Diversify Your Sources: Don't rely on a single news outlet. Read or watch news from multiple sources with different perspectives. This can help you see a more balanced picture of events.
- Check the Source: Consider the credibility of the news outlet. Established media organizations have more rigorous fact-checking processes, although they are not infallible. Be cautious of lesser-known websites, especially those with sensationalist headlines.
- Look for Original Reporting: Primary sources and original reporting are more reliable than articles that aggregate information from other news sources. Investigative journalism that involves firsthand accounts and direct evidence is generally more trustworthy.
- Be Skeptical of Sensationalism: If a story seems too shocking or outrageous to be true, it's worth investigating further. Sensa-

tional headlines are designed to attract attention and may not accurately reflect the content of the article.

- Verify the Story/News against Your Own Moral Code and Principles: Does this pass the "smell test"? Trust your own instincts.
- Understand the Limits of Headlines: Headlines are often crafted to be attention-grabbing and may not provide a complete picture of the story. Always read beyond the headline to understand the full context.
- Be Mindful of Your Own Biases: Everyone has biases that can influence how they interpret information. Being aware of your biases and actively seeking out differing viewpoints can help you form a more balanced understanding.

In an era where information is abundant and easily accessible, the ability to critically evaluate news is more important than ever. By approaching news with a discerning eye, diversifying your sources, and understanding the influence of bias and sensationalism, you can navigate the media landscape more effectively. Remember, don't believe everything you see on the news—take the time to seek out the truth amid the noise.

"God, I want a refund" from all the false and negative information I've consumed over the years. It's time to make space for truth and knowledge.

(Moving forward, I'm not going to include any more one through six steps at the end of chapters. I would encourage you to read back and write some down for yourself. This will help you to do your own research.)

"Don't believe everything you hear: Real eyes, realize, real lies."
—*Tupac Shakur*

# CHAPTER 15
# DON'T WISH YOUR LIFE AWAY

We've all been there—stuck in the grind of the week, and the only glimmer of hope seems to be the approaching weekend. "Is it Friday yet?" Mondays, on the other hand, are often met with groans and reluctance, signaling the end of freedom and the start of responsibilities. But what if we could shift our perspective and find value in every day rather than wishing our lives away?

Do you ever wake up and think to yourself, "Is it Friday yet? I'm so over this week."

Don't do that.

I stood in my office at the City of Southaven's utility department, staring at the calendar on the wall. I marked off another day, my heart lifting slightly as I did. Four years left. Four years until retirement. It couldn't get here fast enough.

Every day felt like a marathon. The early mornings, the endless phone calls, and the constant demands from the public—it was all a grind. The job, which had once been a source of pride and purpose, had become a relentless, exhausting routine. I found myself saying, "I've only got four years left," hoping the repetition would make time speed up.

On a particularly grueling Wednesday, I sat at my desk, sifting through yet another stack of complaints. I glanced at the clock, counting the hours until I could go home and unwind. My mind drifted to my passions, the things that made me feel alive: writing, playing guitar, and spending time with my family.

That evening, I decided to do something different. Instead of watching TV to numb the stress of the day, I picked up my Les Paul. The familiar weight of the guitar in my hands brought a sense of comfort. As I strummed the strings, a melody emerged: "Free Bird," a reflection of my longing for freedom and my hope for the future. The music flowed, taking me to a place where the pressures of work didn't exist, where I was free to express myself fully.

The next day at work, I felt a bit lighter. I still had four years to go, but playing the guitar the night before had reminded me that there were parts of my life that were fulfilling and joyful. I decided to make more time for those things, to bring a piece of my passion into my daily routine.

During my lunch break, I began jotting down ideas for this book. I wrote about overcoming childhood circumstances, about the lessons I learned from my father, and about the importance of emotional connection in relationships. These stories, these reflections, gave me a sense of purpose that went beyond my job.

As the months passed, my mindset began to shift. I still counted down the days to retirement, but I no longer saw my job as a burden to endure. Instead, it was a means to an end, a part of my journey that would lead to the freedom I craved. I found ways to infuse my workdays with moments of creativity and connection, and I started sharing my writing with my colleagues, who appreciated my insights and stories.

One day, a coworker approached me, saying, "Robert, I've been reading your book excerpts. They're really inspiring. I never knew you went through so much. It's given me a new perspective on my own struggles."

I smiled, feeling a sense of fulfillment that had nothing to do with my job title. I realized that my experiences, both the good and the challenging, were valuable. They could help others and provide a sense of connection and understanding.

The years continue to pass, and as my retirement date draws closer, I feel a mix of excitement and gratitude. I look forward to the day retirement will come, but I also appreciate the journey that is leading me there. The job that I once dreaded has become a part of my story, a chapter that is rich with growth and discovery. I have a family here. Our late director, Chris, would always say, "Hey, slick, don't stress over the small things. That's my job," and "I've got your back."

## The Monday Dread

Mondays have an infamous reputation. They're the unwelcome alarm clock that interrupts our restful weekends, pulling us back into the cycle of work and obligations. It's easy to fall into the trap of hating Mondays, but this negativity sets the tone for the entire week. By dreading Mondays, we create a mental block that makes it harder to see the potential each day holds.

Instead of dreading the start of the week, try to reframe Mondays as a fresh beginning. It's a new opportunity to set goals, tackle challenges, and make progress. Embrace the idea that each Monday is a chance to start anew, to take steps toward your ambitions, and to learn something new.

## The Longing for Friday

As the week progresses, the anticipation of Friday can become almost palpable. "Is it Friday yet?" is a common refrain, symbolizing a countdown to freedom and relaxation. But constantly yearning for the weekend means we're not fully living in the present. We miss out on the experiences, interactions, and opportunities that each day offers.

Consider this: there are five weekdays and only two days of the weekend. If we only look forward to those two days, we're wishing away more than half of our lives. Finding joy in the weekdays can transform how we perceive time. Engage more deeply in your daily activities, seek out small pleasures, and cultivate a mindset that values each moment.

## The Power of Perspective

Perspective is a powerful tool. The way we view our days can dramatically affect our overall happiness and satisfaction. If we see weekdays as mere obstacles to overcome, they will indeed feel burdensome. However, if we approach each day with curiosity and a willingness to find meaning, we can change our experience entirely.

Set small, achievable goals for each day. Celebrate your successes, no matter how minor they might seem. Find joy in routine activities and appreciate the little things. This shift in perspective can turn mundane tasks into meaningful experiences and help you see value in every day, not just the weekends.

## Living in the Moment

Living in the moment is about being present and fully engaged with where you are and what you're doing. It's about appreciating the journey rather than just focusing on the destination. Mindfulness practices, such as meditation and conscious breathing, can help cultivate this sense of presence.

When you catch yourself longing for the weekend or dreading Monday, take a moment to pause and reflect. Ask yourself what you can appreciate about the present moment. Maybe it's a conversation with a colleague, a task that brings you satisfaction, or simply the act of being alive and capable.

## Finding Balance

It's natural to look forward to weekends and to feel a bit of reluctance on Mondays. But finding a balance is key. Allow yourself to enjoy the anticipation of the weekend, but don't let it overshadow the rest of the week. Embrace Mondays as a new start rather than an end to your freedom.

Plan activities during the week that you enjoy, whether it's a hobby, a workout, or spending time with loved ones. These moments of joy can break up the week and provide a sense of balance. By creating a fulfilling weekday routine, you reduce the urge to constantly wish for the weekend.

Life is too short to be wished away. Every day, whether it's a Monday or a Friday, has something to offer. By shifting our perspective and finding value in each moment, we can live more fully and joyfully. Embrace the present, set meaningful goals, and appreciate the journey. After all, life is happening right now, not just on the weekends.

Don't let the sadness of your past and the fear of your future ruin the happiness of your present. "God, I want a refund" from every time I've wished yesterday away and overlooked the beauty of today.

"The trick is to enjoy life. Don't wish away your days, waiting for better ones ahead"
-Marjorie Pay Hinckley

# CHAPTER 16
# LOVE IN THE HOUSE OF THE KING

## A Love Story

I worked for Graceland for five years, working on the maintenance and utilities crew of the grand estate. Every day, I marveled at the history and the legend of Elvis Presley that permeated every corner of the mansion. It was a job I loved, allowing me to blend my technical skills with my passion for the King of Rock and Roll.

Natalie, a tour guide, had always been enchanted by Elvis's music. Her job was guiding visitors through Graceland, sharing stories and moments from Elvis's life. She had just started her first day, eager and nervous, hoping to make a good impression.

Our paths crossed in the Hall of Gold. I was fixing a light fixture when Natalie walked in, preparing for her first tour. She paused, watching me work.

"Need a hand?" she offered with a friendly smile.

I looked down from the ladder, surprised but pleased by the interruption. "I think I've got it, but thanks. First day?"

"Yeah," Natalie admitted, tucking a strand of hair behind her ear. "Just trying to soak it all in."

"Welcome aboard," I said, climbing down the ladder. "I'm Robert."

"Natalie," she replied, shaking my hand.

From that moment on, we found ourselves crossing paths more often. I would finish a repair just as Natalie was starting a tour, and we would exchange stories and laughs. We bonded over our love for Elvis's music and our mutual dedication to preserving his legacy.

As weeks turned into months, our friendship blossomed into something deeper. We shared lunches, explored Memphis together, and spent evenings talking about our dreams and aspirations. Our connection was undeniable, a harmony that resonated like the chords of an Elvis song.

One evening after the last tour had ended, I asked Natalie to join me in the Jungle Room. It was our favorite spot, a place where we had shared many moments. As we stood there, surrounded by the vibrant decor, I took her hand.

"I've fallen in love with you, Natalie," I confessed, my voice trembling slightly. "I can't imagine my life without you."

Natalie smiled, tears in her eyes. "I love you, too, Robert."

Years later, we stood together at our wedding, surrounded by friends, family, and our work colleagues. The reception was held in a beautifully decorated hall.

When it was time for our first dance, the familiar melody of "Can't Help Falling in Love" began to play. As the opening chords filled the room, Natalie and I took to the dance floor, our eyes locked on each other. We moved gracefully, lost in the moment, the world around us fading away.

Elvis's voice, rich and timeless, enveloped us, and we felt as if he were singing just for us. The song captured our journey perfectly, a testament to the love that had grown in the heart of Graceland.

As we danced, we knew we were part of something special. Our love story, born in the house of the King, was as enduring and magical as the music that had brought us together. And in that moment, as we swayed to the melody, we knew we would cherish each other forever and ever.

I know what you're thinking: how does a chapter about how I met my wife really help anyone? Well, I'll tell you. I didn't want to write a chapter about relationships without first telling y'all a little bit about how I met my wife. Also, you can refer back to the "Answer is Always No If You Don't Ask" chapter. I try to think about how my life would be today if I never would've taken the first step and just asked her on our first date. The fear of rejection can be paralyzing. It's easier to stay in your comfort zone, to not take the risk. So I asked her out on a date. Looking back now, I realize how pivotal that moment was. If I had let my fear hold me back, I wouldn't have experienced the joy and love that Natalie has brought into my life. Our relationship grew stronger with each passing day, and we faced life's challenges together, always supporting one another. Writing this chapter isn't just about telling you a love story; it's about illustrating the importance of taking that first step, of not letting fear dictate your actions. It's about understanding that the greatest opportunities in life often come from the risks we're willing to take. In relationships, as in life, the answer is always no if you don't ask. If you never put yourself out there, you'll never know what incredible experiences you might be missing. So, take that chance. Ask the question. You might just find the love of your life, as I did with Natalie. And in doing so, you'll learn that the first step is often the hardest, but it's also the most rewarding.

"Don't forget what happened to the man who suddenly got everything
he ever wanted."
"What happened?"
"He lived happily ever after."
—*Mr. Wonka*

# CHAPTER 17
# THE COMPLEXITIES OF RELATIONSHIPS

## Introduction

Relationships are the bedrock of human experience. They shape who we are, influence our decisions, and provide the support systems we rely on throughout our lives. Whether familial, romantic, or platonic, relationships are a complex weaving of emotions, expectations, and interactions. Understanding the dynamics of relationships can help us navigate them more effectively and create more meaningful connections.

## The Foundation of Relationships

At their core, relationships are built on communication, trust, and mutual respect. Communication is the lifeline of any relationship, allowing individuals to express their needs, share their thoughts, and resolve conflicts. Trust is the glue that holds relationships together, fostering a sense of security and reliability. Mutual respect ensures that each person's boundaries, feelings, and individuality are honored.

## Against All Odds

In every journey, there are moments of doubt and uncertainty. For me and my spouse, the path was no different. Life threw numerous challenges our way, and more than once, we found ourselves questioning whether we could overcome them. The thought, "I don't think we're going to make it" echoed in our hearts during the toughest times. But through perseverance, love, and unwavering support for each other, we always found a way to rise above the adversity.

The first major challenge came shortly after I lost my job at Graceland. The sudden shift in my career put a strain on our finances and our emotional well-being. The stress of adjusting to a lower income, coupled with the blow to my pride, created a tense atmosphere at home. There were nights when I sat at the kitchen table, bills spread out before me, and wondered aloud if I could keep my head above water.

"I don't think we're going to make it," I admitted one evening, my voice heavy with worry. My spouse reached across the table and took my hand. "We'll get through this together," she said. My determination to prove myself at my new job with the city paid off, and with careful budgeting, it helped us stay afloat until my promotion to crew foreman. Twenty-one years later, I'm now the utilities supervisor.

I refused to give up. I worked tirelessly, often late into the night. We leaned on each other for strength and encouragement, never letting the weight of our doubts crush our spirits.

Looking back, I can see how far my spouse and I have come. Every moment of doubt, every time we said, "I don't think we're going to make it," only strengthened our bond and our resolve. We faced financial struggles, career challenges, and the uncertainties of starting a business, yet we emerged stronger and more united.

Our journey was a powerful reminder that no matter how daunting the challenges, we could overcome anything as long as we faced it together. The promise we made to each other—to always believe and support one another—carried us through the darkest times.

"You and your spouse can do this," we often tell others now, drawing from our own experiences. "I promise." Our story is a beacon of hope for those facing their own struggles, a testament to the power of perseverance, love, and unwavering support. Against all odds, we made it, and our journey will continue to inspire others to believe that they can too.

## The Stages of Relationships

Relationships often evolve through several stages:

- Acquaintance: The initial stage where individuals meet and get to know each other. First impressions play a significant role here, and common interests often act as a catalyst for further inter-action.

- Building: As individuals spend more time together, they build a deeper understanding of each other. This stage involves sharing experiences, discovering shared values, and developing a sense of trust.
- Commitment: In romantic relationships, this stage might involve declaring exclusivity or making long-term plans. In friendships, it might mean a deeper bond where both parties are invested in each other's well-being.
- Maintenance: Relationships require ongoing effort to sustain. Regular communication, acts of kindness, and addressing con-flicts are crucial for maintaining a healthy relationship.
- Growth or Decline: Relationships either grow stronger or weak-en over time. Growth is marked by increased intimacy and mu-tual support, while decline can result from unresolved conflicts, lack of communication, or divergent paths.

## The Role of Communication

Effective communication is the cornerstone of any successful rela-tionship. It involves not just speaking but also listening actively. Here are some key aspects:

- Active Listening: Paying full attention, understanding the mes-sage, and responding thoughtfully.
- Nonverbal Communication: Body language, facial expressions, and eye contact can convey emotions and intentions more pow-erfully than words.
- Honesty and Openness: Being truthful and transparent fosters trust and reduces misunderstandings.
- Empathy: Understanding and sharing the feelings of another en-hances emotional connection and support.

## Conflict Resolution

Conflicts are inevitable in any relationship. How they are managed can strengthen or weaken the bond. Effective conflict resolution in-volves:

- Staying Calm: Maintaining composure helps in addressing the issue rationally rather than emotionally.
- Identifying the Issue: Clearly defining the problem helps in finding a resolution.
- Collaborative Approach: Working together to find a solution helps reach one that satisfies both parties.
- Forgiveness: Letting go of grudges and resentments is essential for moving forward.
- **The Influence of External Factors**
- External factors such as social, economic, and cultural influences can impact relationships. Understanding these influences helps in navigating challenges:
- Cultural Norms: Different cultures have varying expectations and practices regarding relationships. Being aware of these differences can prevent misunderstandings.
- Economic Pressure: Financial stress can strain relationships. Open discussions about finances and shared responsibilities can mitigate this.
- Social Media: While it can enhance connection, it can also create unrealistic expectations and comparisons. Balancing online and offline interactions is crucial.

## The Importance of Self-Care

Maintaining a healthy relationship starts with taking care of oneself. Self-care involves:

- Emotional Well-Being: Managing stress, expressing emotions healthily, and seeking support when needed are essential for emotional wellness.
- Physical Health: Regular exercise, a balanced diet, and adequate sleep contribute to overall well-being.
- Personal Growth: Pursuing hobbies, goals, and interests outside the relationship enriches one's life and brings new energy to the relationship.

## Sharing the Load—Helping Out to Foster Intimacy

Men, this is for you, so pay very close attention to what I'm about to say. Guys, have you ever felt frustrated, wondering why your wife or girlfriend wasn't as eager for intimacy as you are?

When we think about relationships and intimacy, it's crucial to understand the daily dynamics that shape our interactions and expectations. Imagine a day in the life of your partner—working tirelessly, managing the kids, keeping the household in order. By the end of such a day, her energy is depleted, her patience stretched thin, and the last thing on her mind might be intimacy.

The last thing a woman wants after a long, exhausting day is to feel pressured for intimacy. Instead, she needs to feel seen, heard, and supported. By stepping up, sharing responsibilities, and building a strong emotional connection, you create a foundation for a deeper, more fulfilling relationship. So men, help out. Not just to foster intimacy, but to build a partnership based on love, respect, and mutual support.

Also try to imagine this scenario: every time you make love, she gets to enjoy a delicious steak dinner, but all you get is a single cold French fry. How would you feel? That's how they feel sometimes when you're intimate. They love you, but they need more than just a cold French fry. They need to feel cherished, appreciated, and satisfied too.

(As a heads-up, this part has sensitive material.) I won't go into details, but achieving full intimacy requires both partners to feel fulfilled every time. This is a realistic and empowering goal. It requires understanding one's own body, effective communication with a partner, and a willingness to explore and experiment. By addressing physical and relational factors, women can enhance their experiences and achieve greater satisfaction. Remember, the journey to greater intimacy and mutual fulfillment is ongoing. It is personal and unique to each individual, and there is no one-size-fits-all approach. With patience, openness, and effort, every woman can reach the heights of greater intimacy and mutual satisfaction. The key lies in open communication, trust, and a genuine desire to understand and meet each other's needs.

- Open communication about desires, fantasies, and what feels good is crucial.
- Verbal communication—clearly expressing likes and dislikes—is important.
- Nonverbal cues (body language) also play a key role.

**Emotional Connection**

An emotional bond with a partner can enhance sexual satisfaction:

- Building Trust: Feeling safe and connected with a partner can reduce inhibitions.
- Intimacy: Forms of intimacy like cuddling and kissing can enhance the overall connection and pave the way for better experiences.

Relationships are intricate and multifaceted, requiring effort, understanding, and a willingness to grow both individually and together. By fostering effective communication, resolving conflicts, understanding external influences, and prioritizing self-care, we can build and maintain healthy, fulfilling relationships. In the end, the quality of our relationships significantly contributes to the richness of our lives.

Life often feels like a series of transactions, where we invest our time, heart, and energy.

"God, I want a refund" from every argument and lost moments spent in misunderstanding and miscommunication.

"Why would you want to marry me for, anyhow?"
"So I can kiss you anytime I want."
—*Sweet Home Alabama*

# CHAPTER 18
# LET'S STAY HUMBLE

In a world that often rewards brash confidence and self-promotion, humility might seem like a relic of the past. Yet humility remains a cornerstone of genuine leadership, deep relationships, and personal growth. To stay humble is not to deny one's achievements or potential but to recognize the value and contributions of others and to remain open to learning and growth.

## The Power of Humility

Humility is often misunderstood as weakness or low self-esteem, but true humility is a sign of strength. It means having a clear perspective, understanding one's limitations, and appreciating the worth of others. Humility allows for the acknowledgment that no one person has all the answers or possesses every skill. This mindset fosters collaboration, encourages diverse viewpoints, and leads to more innovative solutions.

## Redemption and Resilience

Michael had always been a dedicated and skilled service technician for the Southaven Water Department. His work and unwavering commitment had earned him the position of lead service technician. For years, he managed a team of technicians, ensuring that the city's water systems ran smoothly. His reputation for reliability and expertise made him a respected figure among his peers.

But life has a way of throwing unexpected challenges, and for Michael, it was a series of unfortunate events that led to his demotion. It was a difficult period; the demotion was a blow to his pride and his career. He was now back on the ground level, working alongside the very crew he used to lead. The transition was tough, but Michael was determined not to let this setback define him.

Instead of wallowing in disappointment, Michael saw his demotion as an opportunity to prove his worth once again. He threw himself into his work with renewed vigor, showing the same level of dedication and attention to detail that had once earned him his leadership role. His resilience did not go unnoticed. Colleagues and supervisors alike saw his determination and the quality of his work. Over time, he earned their respect and trust once again.

Slowly but surely, Michael began to climb the ranks. His consistency and hard work paid off when he was promoted to crew foreman. In this role, he demonstrated exceptional leadership, guiding his team through challenging projects and ensuring the smooth operation of the city's water systems. Michael's journey back to a leadership position was a testament to his character and work ethic.

However, Michael's ambitions didn't stop at the water department. He had always harbored a passion for helping others in more immediate, impactful ways. This passion led him to pursue a career as a firefighter. Balancing his duties as a crew foreman with the rigorous training required to become a firefighter was no easy feat, but Michael was no stranger to hard work and perseverance.

After months of intensive training, Michael achieved his goal. He was now a firefighter, ready to serve and protect the community in a new capacity. The transition to firefighting was seamless for him; the skills he had honed in the water department, such as problem-solving, teamwork, and leadership, proved invaluable in his new role.

As Michael settled into his new career, he also decided to pursue another long-held dream: owning his own business. Drawing on his extensive experience in water services, he established a small side business. His reputation and connections within the city helped his business grow quickly.

Today, Michael is not just a respected firefighter but is also successful with his side business. His story is a powerful reminder that setbacks are not the end but rather a part of the journey. Through hard work, perseverance, and an unwavering commitment to his goals, Michael transformed challenges into opportunities, carving out a life of purpose and fulfillment.

## The Benefits of Being Humble

*Personal Growth*

Humble individuals are more open to feedback and criticism, which are essential for personal development. They view mistakes as opportunities to learn rather than as failures.

*Building Trust*

People are naturally drawn to those who are modest and genuine. Humility builds trust because it shows authenticity and a willingness to prioritize others over oneself.

*Stronger Relationships*

Humble people tend to be better listeners and more empathetic, which enhances their relationships. By valuing others' opinions and feelings, they create deeper, more meaningful connections.

*Leadership*

Humble leaders inspire loyalty and respect. They empower their teams by acknowledging their contributions and encouraging a collaborative environment.

## Cultivating Humility

Humility is a practice, not a fixed trait. It requires constant self-reflection and a willingness to grow. Here are some ways to cultivate humility:

- Seek Feedback: Regularly ask for feedback from colleagues, friends, and family. Listen to their perspectives without becoming defensive.
- Acknowledge Others: Give credit where it's due. Celebrate the achievements of others and recognize their contributions to your success.

- Practice Gratitude: Keep a gratitude journal to remind yourself of the positive aspects of your life and the people who support you.
- Stay Curious: Approach life with a learner's mindset. Be curious about others' experiences and viewpoints and be willing to admit when you don't know something.
- Serve Others: Engage in acts of service, whether through volunteering or simply helping those around you. Serving others helps keep your ego in check and reminds you of the larger community you are part of.

## Stories of Humility

History is replete with examples of humble leaders and figures who have left lasting impacts. Consider Mahatma Gandhi, who led India to independence through a philosophy of nonviolence and humility. Despite his significant influence, Gandhi lived simply and maintained a deep respect for all individuals.

Another example is Nelson Mandela, who, after spending twenty-seven years in prison, emerged with a spirit of reconciliation rather than revenge. His humility and willingness to forgive were pivotal in leading South Africa toward unity and healing.

## The Balance of Humility and Confidence

Humility does not mean downplaying your abilities or achievements. It's about maintaining a balance where you recognize your strengths and contributions while staying open to learning from others and acknowledging their value. Confidence and humility can coexist. When combined, they create a powerful force that leads to authentic leadership and personal fulfillment.

Staying humble is a lifelong journey that enriches our lives and the lives of those around us. It requires us to look beyond ourselves, embrace our imperfections, and continually strive to grow and contribute to the greater good. In a world that often emphasizes self-promotion, choosing humility can be a radical act of strength and wisdom. So let's stay humble, recognizing that our true power lies in our ability to learn, connect, and uplift others.

"God, I want a refund" from every time I let my pride cloud my judgment. True humility allows us to be more receptive, more in tune with others, and ultimately, more effective in our endeavors.

"Stay humble. Always answer your phone—no matter who else is in the car."

—*Jack Lemmon*

# CHAPTER 19
## REBUILDING BRIDGES

While I was growing up, my father was a hard worker and tried his best to provide for us. Yet beneath that magnetic exterior lay a tumultuous struggle with addiction that often threatened to tear our family apart. Each time he burned a bridge with his erratic behavior, it fell to me to mend it, no matter how deep the scars ran. Because he was my father—and despite his flaws—I couldn't abandon him.

My earliest memories of my father are bittersweet. There were moments of warmth and laughter, where his love felt like a protective shield against the world. But those moments were fleeting, overshadowed by his unpredictable outbursts and absences. His addiction to drugs created a chasm between the man he could be and the man he was. As a child, I couldn't fully grasp the gravity of his addiction, but I understood its impact on our lives.

Every relapse was a new blaze that consumed the fragile bridges we had painstakingly built. He would disappear for days, sometimes weeks, leaving a trail of broken promises and shattered hopes.

In the midst of this chaos, I found myself becoming a mediator, a bridge builder. When my father would return, often remorseful and seeking forgiveness, it was my job to pick up the pieces. I would listen to his apologies, comfort my mother, and try to restore some semblance of normalcy. It wasn't just about mending relationships; it was about preserving the love I had for him, a love that was tested but never extinguished.

There were countless times I wanted to walk away, to let the bridges burn and leave the wreckage behind. The pain and disappointment were overwhelming, and it seemed unfair that I had to shoulder such a burden. But each time I reached that breaking point, I would remember the moments of tenderness, the glimpses of the father he could be. It was those memories that fueled my determination to keep rebuilding, no matter how many times the bridges collapsed.

As I grew older, I began to understand addiction better. I learned that my father's actions were not entirely his own; they were driven by a disease that he struggled to control. This realization didn't excuse his behavior, but it gave me a new perspective. I saw him not just as the man who hurt us but as someone who was hurting too. It was this empathy that strengthened my resolve to keep the lines of communication open, to offer support even when it felt undeserved.

Rebuilding bridges wasn't just about forgiveness; it was about hope. Hope that one day my father would conquer his demons and become the man he aspired to be. Hope that our family could heal and move forward together. Each act of rebuilding was a testament to the belief that love could overcome even the deepest wounds.

There were times of progress when my father would stay clean for months and our family would start to heal. These periods were fragile but precious, offering a glimpse of the life we could have. I cherished these times, using them as motivation to keep fighting for him, for us. But addiction is a relentless adversary, and setbacks were inevitable. Each relapse felt like a betrayal, yet I knew that abandoning him was not an option.

In the end, rebuilding those bridges wasn't just about saving my father; it was about saving myself. It was about holding on to the belief that people can change, that love and perseverance can make a difference. It was about proving to myself that I could rise above the circumstances that tried to hold me back. And it was about honoring the man who, despite his flaws, was still my father.

Rebuilding bridges with my father taught me resilience, compassion, and the power of unconditional love. It showed me that even in the darkest times, there is always a flicker of light worth nurturing. And while our journey was fraught with pain and setbacks, it also brought moments of profound connection and understanding. In the end, those bridges we rebuilt together became the foundation of a bond that, despite everything, could not be broken.

## The Last Goodbye

My father's battle with addiction was a long and arduous journey, one that eventually claimed his life. He died of liver failure, his body unable to withstand the years of abuse it had endured. Despite the pain and turmoil that had marked our relationship, his passing left a void that words could scarcely fill. Our last conversation, strangely enough, was a moment of unexpected poignancy, marked by a quote from the movie *Tombstone*.

The final months of my father's life were a painful descent. His health deteriorated rapidly. We both knew the end was near, though neither of us wanted to say it out loud. There were unspoken truths, lingering regrets, and a deep sense of loss that permeated our interactions.

During one of my visits to the hospital, we found ourselves reminiscing about better times, trying to find solace in shared memories. Movies were one of the few escapes we had enjoyed together, a brief respite from the chaos of our lives. *Tombstone* was one of his favorites, a film we had watched countless times. Its themes of loyalty, redemption, and friendship resonated with him, perhaps more deeply than I ever realized.

As we talked, my father seemed to gather some of his old spirit. His eyes, though dimmed by illness, lit up as he recounted scenes from the movie. It was during this conversation that he looked at me, his voice weak but clear, and quoted one of the film's most memorable lines: "I'm your huckleberry." It was a quote from Doc Holliday, a character who, despite his flaws and illnesses, remained fiercely loyal to his friends.

In that moment, I understood what my father was trying to convey. It was his way of telling me that, despite everything, he had always cared for me and always tried to be there in his own way. It was an acknowledgment of our bond, imperfect yet unbreakable. Those four words carried the weight of a lifetime of unspoken emotions, a final attempt to bridge the gap between us.

Our conversation drifted after that, touching on less significant matters, but those words lingered in the air. They were a poignant reminder of the man my father was at his core, beneath the layers of addiction and pain. He was flawed, yes, but he was also someone who loved deeply, even if he couldn't always show it in the ways that mattered most.

In the days that followed, I found myself replaying that conversation over and over in my mind as his condition worsened. The simplicity of the quote belied its significance, encapsulating the essence of our relationship. It was a testament to the moments of connection we had managed to salvage from the wreckage of our lives, a final gift from a father to his son.

When my father passed away, I felt an overwhelming sense of grief, mingled with a strange sense of relief. His suffering was over, but so, too, was the chance for any further reconciliation. The bridges we had built, burned, and rebuilt countless times now stood as monuments to our shared history. His last words to me were not a grand declaration or an apology but a simple quote from a beloved movie, one that captured the essence of our complicated bond.

In the wake of his death, I found solace in those words. They became a touchstone, a way to remember my father not just for his flaws but for the moments of genuine connection we shared. "I'm your huckleberry" was more than a line from a film; it was a promise of loyalty, a declaration of love that transcended the pain and disappointment.

My father's passing taught me many things about forgiveness, resilience, and the enduring power of love. It showed me that even in the face of insurmountable odds, there is always room for reconciliation, for understanding. And it reminded me that the bonds we forge with those we love, no matter how fraught with difficulty, are worth fighting for.

In the end, my father's legacy was not defined by his addiction but by the moments of connection we managed to find amid the turmoil. His last words to me, a simple quote from *Tombstone*, encapsulated the essence of our relationship: flawed, complicated, but ultimately bound by love. And that, I realized, was a bridge that could never be burned.

### Knowing When to Let Go

Sometimes, despite our best efforts, a relationship cannot be salvaged. In these cases, it's important to know when to let go and move forward.

*Recognizing Toxicity*

If a relationship consistently brings more harm than good, it may be time to let go. Toxic relationships drain energy, hinder growth, and impact mental health. Prioritize your well-being.

*Acceptance*

Accept that not all relationships are meant to last. People grow and change, and some relationships may no longer serve a positive purpose in your life.

*Moving Forward*

Focus on building new bridges and nurturing positive relationships. Learn from past experiences and apply those lessons to future interactions.

While some bridges are better left in ashes, others may be worth the effort to rebuild. The key lies in understanding the value of each relationship, knowing when to fight for it, and when to let go for the sake of your own growth and happiness.

"God, I want a refund" from every bridge I've burned and every mistake I've made. I want a refund for all the pain I've endured and the tears I've shed.

"Love can build a bridge / Between your heart and mine / Love can build a bridge / Don't you think it's time? / Don't you think it's time?"
—*The Judds*

# CHAPTER 20
# WHERE DO WE GO FROM HERE?

Life is a series of transitions. Each phase, each chapter, brings with it its own set of challenges, joys, and lessons. As we navigate through these moments, we often find ourselves at a crossroads, wondering, "Where do we go from here?" This question is not just about direction; it's about purpose, growth, and the journey toward becoming the best version of ourselves.

In my journey, this question has come up time and again. After overcoming the adversities of childhood and rebuilding relationships shattered by my parents' addictions, I have often found myself standing at the edge of the unknown. The path ahead isn't always clear, but the steps we take now can shape the future in profound ways.

## Moving Forward No Matter What

Life has a way of leaving marks on us, both visible and invisible. These scars, whether they are physical reminders of past injuries or emotional wounds from life's many battles, are part of our journey. They serve as evidence of our survival, our resilience, and our growth. But they do not define us; rather, they remind us of where we have been and who we have become. Moving forward despite these scars is not just a choice—it's a necessity.

Scars remind us of our past and who we are, but they don't change us. Instead, they tell a story of endurance and strength. Each scar carries a tale of a challenge faced and overcome, a moment when giving up was not an option. For me, the scars of my past, particularly those involving my father and his struggles with addiction, have shaped my perspective on life and resilience.

Moving forward requires an unyielding determination not to let our scars dictate our path. It means acknowledging the pain but refusing to be paralyzed by it. It involves embracing the lessons our scars teach us and using them as fuel to propel us toward a better future.

We are all shaped by our experiences, but we are not defined by them. "God, I want a refund" for the years stolen by bitterness and grief. Instead, I will invest in the years ahead with hope and resilience.

Scars are reminders that we are human, that we have lived and experienced life in all its harshness and beauty. They are not marks of shame but badges of honor, symbols of our capacity to endure and grow. Moving forward, no matter what, is about embracing our scars and allowing them to be part of our narrative—but not the whole story.

Every day is a new opportunity to step forward, to take the lessons from our scars and use them to build a future that is not dictated by our past but informed by it. We are not the sum of our wounds but the strength we have gained from healing. So no matter what, keep moving forward. The journey ahead is shaped not by where we have been but by the determination and hope with which we step into the future.

## Embracing Uncertainty

The first step in moving forward is embracing uncertainty. Life doesn't come with a road map, and that's OK. The uncertainty can be daunting, but it's also a blank canvas, offering limitless possibilities. Instead of fearing the unknown, we can choose to see it as an adventure, an opportunity to explore, learn, and grow.

## Setting Intentions

Having a clear intention is crucial. Intentions are different from goals. Goals are specific and measurable, while intentions are about overall direction and purpose. They are the guiding principles that keep us aligned with our values and dreams. When we set our intentions, we create a compass that helps us navigate through life's complexities.

For me, my intentions have always centered around growth, connection, and authenticity. Whether it's in my personal relationships, my work with the City of Southaven, or my writing, I strive to stay true to these core principles. They have helped me stay grounded, even when the path ahead seemed uncertain.

## Taking Action

Intentions are powerful, but they must be accompanied by action. It's easy to get stuck in the planning phase, waiting for the perfect moment or the ideal conditions. But the truth is there will never be a perfect time. We have to take the first step, even if it's a small one. Action creates momentum, and momentum propels us forward.

In my life, taking action has often meant stepping out of my comfort zone. It has meant having difficult conversations, making tough decisions, and facing my fears head-on. But every time I took a step forward, no matter how small, I found that the path became a little clearer.

## Learning from the Past

Our past holds valuable lessons. Reflecting on where we've been can give us insights into where we want to go. It's important to acknowledge the experiences that have shaped us, the mistakes we've made, and the wisdom we've gained. By understanding our past, we can avoid repeating patterns that no longer serve us and make more informed choices moving forward.

My past, with all its challenges and triumphs, has taught me resilience, empathy, and the importance of forgiveness. It has shown me that while we can't change what has happened, we have the power to change how we respond and how we grow from it.

## Building a Support System

No journey is meant to be taken alone. Having a support system can make all the difference. Whether it's family, friends, mentors, or a community, the people we surround ourselves with can provide encouragement, perspective, and accountability.

In my life, the support of my wife, my colleagues, and my close friends has been invaluable. They have lifted me up in times of doubt, celebrated my successes, and offered wisdom when I needed it most.

Building and nurturing these relationships has been a key part of my journey.

## Looking Ahead

When we ask, "Where do we go from here?" as we stand at the crossroads of our lives, we must remember that the answer lies within us. It's in our intentions, our actions, our reflections, and our connections. The path ahead may be uncertain, but it's also filled with potential and possibility.

For me, the journey continues with a commitment to growth, a dedication to building meaningful relationships, and a passion for making a positive impact in my community and beyond. It's about moving forward with purpose and embracing the adventure that lies ahead.

I have always believed that if my book could help just one person, all my effort would be worth it. As I sit here at my house, surrounded by notes and drafts, I feel a sense of purpose and hope. This book is more than just a collection of stories—it is a testament to resilience, forgiveness, and the power of personal growth.

Writing about overcoming childhood circumstances, rebuilding relationships, and understanding the complexities of human connections has been a therapeutic journey for me. I want readers to find solace in my experiences and to see that, despite the challenges, there was always a way forward.

Throughout my life, I faced not only emotional challenges but significant health struggles as well. There were times when my health issues were so bad, I didn't think I was going to make it, making it difficult to maintain a positive outlook. Yet these experiences taught me the importance of perseverance and the strength that comes from facing challenges head-on.

I have often thought about my time working at Elvis Presley's Graceland. Those five years were filled with unique experiences and countless stories. I've even been upstairs and can remember every detail. My wife made me write it all down years ago. I have seen the magic of the place through the eyes of thousands of visitors, each with their own connection to the King of Rock and Roll. The memories of Graceland, both the humorous and the profound, are vivid in my mind.

One particular memory stands out. It was the day a family from Europe visited Graceland. They were avid Elvis fans, and their excitement was contagious. As they made their way through the mansion, sharing stories and anecdotes, I noticed the youngest child, a boy of about ten, staring at Elvis's guitars with wide-eyed wonder. The boy's father explained that his son had just started learning to play the guitar and idolized Elvis.

I asked, "You like guitars?"

The boy nodded enthusiastically. "Yeah, I just started learning to play."

"Nice to meet you. I'm Robert." I knelt down to be at eye level with the boy. "You know, I started playing guitar around your age."

"Really?" His eyes widened even more. "Was it hard?"

I laughed. "Oh, it was very hard. There were times I wanted to give up. But I had a secret to keep going." I paused, seeing the curiosity in his eyes.

"What was it?" he asked eagerly.

"It's like chopping wood. When you're chopping wood, sometimes you get tired, your hands hurt, and it feels like you'll never get through that big log. But you know what? If you take a break and then come back to it, piece by piece, you'll eventually chop it all away."

The boy nodded slowly, absorbing the metaphor. "So you're saying I should take breaks but never give up?"

"Exactly," I affirmed. "No matter how hard it gets, never give up. Keep practicing, keep playing, and you'll get better. It's OK to take breaks, but always come back and keep chopping away."

The boy's eyes sparkled with even more enthusiasm, and his father looked at me with deep appreciation.

I couldn't help but think of my own father's 1978 Les Paul guitar, still out there somewhere, a symbol of our complicated yet ultimately forgiving relationship. Inspired, I shared the story of my father's guitar with the family.

That moment stayed with me. It was a reminder during the writing process of why I was writing this book. If I could touch even one person's life, inspire one child to follow their dreams, or help someone mend a broken relationship, I would have achieved something truly meaningful.

As I continued to write, I felt a growing excitement for my next project. I envisioned a second book, perhaps an autobiography, where I could dive deeper into my life, including my unforgettable years at Graceland. There were so many stories left to tell—stories of joy, laughter, and the kind spirit of people who found inspiration in Elvis's legacy. This book is just the beginning of many stories to come.

I knew that my journey was just beginning. With each chapter I wrote, I hoped to light a path for others, showing that no matter where you come from or what you've been through, there is always a chance for redemption, growth, and happiness. And if my words could help just one person, I would be eternally grateful.

Thank you for joining me on this journey. May you find strength in your challenges, joy in your achievements, and health in every aspect of your life. Here's to a future filled with vitality, happiness, and endless possibilities.

And don't forget you can always say "God, I want a refund."

"If I leave here tomorrow / would you still remember me?"
—*Ronnie Van Zant*

# ACKNOWLEDGMENTS

This book is dedicated to all my family and friends, especially my wife, Natalie, and my two boys. I wouldn't still be here without you. Thank you, thank you, thank you—for guiding me, for loving me, for believing in me even when I didn't believe in myself.

Natalie, your unwavering support and love have been my anchor through the storms of life. You have been my confidante, my rock, and my inspiration. Your strength and compassion have shown me the true meaning of partnership. My journey hasn't been easy, but with you by my side, it's been worth every struggle.

To our boys, you are my pride and joy. Your laughter, curiosity, and boundless energy remind me every day of the beauty and wonder in the world. Watching you grow has been my greatest privilege, and your presence has given my life purpose and meaning.

To my extended family and friends, your encouragement and faith in me have been the pillars upon which I have built my resilience. You have seen me at my worst and stood by me, offering a helping hand and a listening ear. Your collective strength has carried me through the darkest times, and for that, I am eternally grateful.

This book is not just a reflection of my journey but a testament to the incredible people who have walked beside me. Each page is infused with the love, support, and wisdom you have all generously shared with me. From the bottom of my heart, thank you for being the guiding lights that have illuminated my path.

Let's take one step at a time into the uncertain yet promising tomorrows. But as we step forward, I can't help but feel a deep yearning for more—a desire for fairness, justice, and a sense of completion. Is it wrong for me to feel this way? To want something back from a world that has so often taken more than it has given? No, it's not wrong. It's human to crave balance, to wish for recompense for all we've endured. It's not wrong to seek what seems rightfully deserved.

So where do we go from here? We go forward, with courage, intention, and a heart open to the endless possibilities of what we can become. And remember you can always say, "*God, I want a refund.*"